Letting the Buggers be Crea

Other titles by Sue Cowley:

Getting the Buggers to Think

Getting the Buggers to Behave 2

Getting the Buggers to Write 2

Guerilla Guide to Teaching

How to Survive Your First Year in Teaching

Sue Cowley's Teaching Clinic

Sue Cowley's A–Z of Teaching

Getting your Little Darlings to Behave

Other titles in the Buggers series:

Getting the Buggers into Languages – Amanda Barton

Getting the Buggers into Science – Christine Farmery

Getting the Buggers to Turn Up – Ian McCormack

Getting the Buggers to Add Up – Mike Ollerton

Getting the Buggers to Draw – Barbara Ward

Letting the Buggers be Creative

Sue Cowley

continuum
LONDON • NEW YORK

Continuum International Publishing Group

The Tower Building	15 East 26th Street
11 York Road	New York
London SE1 7NX	NY 10010

www.continuumbooks.com

British Library Cataloguing-in-Publication Data
A catalogue record for this book is available from the British Library.

ISBN: 0–8264–7334–2 (paperback)

Typeset by RefineCatch Limited, Bungay, Suffolk
Printed and bound in Great Britain by
Hobbs The Printers, Hampshire

Contents

To Tilak and Alexandra,
with special thanks to you both
for letting me be creative.

Acknowledgements

Thanks to all the team at Continuum, especially Anthony Haynes, Suzanne Ashley, Katie Sayers, Christina Parkinson and, of course, my editor Alexandra Webster.

Thanks to my mum, who encouraged and nurtured my early creative efforts, and who never complained about sewing endless layers of lace into tutus. Thanks to Tilak for doing all the important administrative bits and pieces that allow me to get on with writing, and to Álvie for reminding me about how creative young children really are.

Finally, a big 'thank you' to the teacher who came to my talk at Methvens Booksellers in Canterbury, and who suggested the original title for this book. It's taken me a while, but here it is!

Introduction

You see things; and you say, 'Why?' But I dream things that never were; and I say, 'Why not?'

George Bernard Shaw

I've got the builders in at the moment. And watching them work, I got to thinking about the nature of creativity (as you do). Of course, building is primarily about skills and techniques – about knowing how to measure materials, mix cement or lay bricks. But as my builders carve out a new room for me, they are certainly using plenty of creativity. This is particularly so when they come up against a problem that needs solving. Let me give you a quick example to show you what I mean.

On removing a bathroom wall, it was discovered that a vital ceiling joist was missing. At this point there was much scratching of heads and tea drinking (often a great way to stir those creative juices). Next there was some talk about having to build a wall right in the middle of the room (umm, no thanks). There was also brief mention of removing the ceiling to insert the joist that should have been there in the first place. (I vetoed that one on the grounds that I was sitting directly above that very ceiling, writing this book.)

Eventually, though, my builder applied a good splash of creativity and came up with an alternative idea. I now have a rather beautiful bar of steel with a curl on the end that does its job (stopping the ceiling from falling down) and which also doubles up as what my builders cunningly call a 'feature'. Since then there has been much humorous discussion of the creative uses to which my steel curl might be put. Various suggestions have been made, from a hanging plant pot holder to some which are just a bit too cheeky to print. Now, I challenge anyone to say that what my builder has done is not a glorious example of creativity. Granted, he's not Shakespeare or Michelangelo, but you get very few of those to the pound. This is a story which has a moral, as all the best stories do. And the moral of this story is that we can *all* be creative, pretty much all of the time: that creativity is as much about an attitude as it is about an activity. Very few of us make a living as artists, or dancers, or musicians, but that doesn't mean we can't be creative in what we do. Creativity is not the sole preserve of the artistic genius – it's something that can and should be available and applicable to every single individual, in almost all aspects of our lives. And so this book is about how we can open the doors to creativity for each and every one of our students, whatever subject we happen to be teaching.

In this book you will find lots of ideas and advice for developing creativity in your classroom, and in your school. With the current emphasis on acquiring skills and passing exams, creativity is in real danger of being crowded out of the curriculum. In this book I show that it is possible to find a place for creativity in every subject, even those which are not traditionally thought of as particularly 'creative' areas of the curriculum. I give a huge range of tips, strategies and suggestions that will assist you in becoming a more creative teacher. Not only will this offer huge benefits for your students, but it will also remind you just how interesting and exciting your job as a teacher can and should be. As with all my books, rather than coming from a theoretical perspective, my aim here has been to give practical advice and realistic strategies that you can actually use.

You'll notice how, throughout the book, I talk about my own creative experiences and thought processes. If you've read any of my other books, you will know that I do like to write from a rather personal perspective. My hope is that, by analysing my own creative journey in this way, I can shine a bit of light onto the way that creativity works. You might also notice that I have scattered a variety of quotations throughout this book. To me, there is something very appealing about quotes. They are little chunks of language that offer a wonderful way of summing up a topic or an impression or an idea. (Although as someone called Richard Kemph memorably said: 'Quotes are nothing but inspiration for the uninspired'!)

All of a sudden, creativity has become the latest buzzword in schools. And after years of topic work being derided as worthless and seen as hopelessly out of fashion, it is finally starting to come back into vogue. The problem with separating subjects out – seeing English as entirely separate from history, or maths as completely disconnected from science – is that we compartmentalize learning into unnatural divisions which simply do not exist in reality. So, now that we've chopped our children's learning up into the constituent bits known as 'the curriculum', we're going to have to stick it all back together again if we really want to encourage creativity.

At this point I'd like to make a plea to those in power, just in case any of them happen to be reading this book. I spend a lot of time going around schools and talking to teachers, and I hear the same request over and over again, particularly at primary level. What teachers want is a bit of space and time to be creative, and to allow their children to be creative as well. Please trust teachers to do their job in the best way that they possibly can, rather than indulging in this constant, unsettling, goal-post moving. Let us be creative in our professional lives, rather than always feeling the need to dictate and detail every moment of every school day.

The vast majority of the teachers that I know are wonderfully creative people. The job itself offers endless opportunities for creativity. You will know of (or hopefully be) one of those brilliant teachers who apply so much commitment and creativity to their work that the students cannot fail to be inspired. It's great fun being a creative teacher – it makes the job seem more like play than like work. Those who aim to be creative do walk a risky, error-strewn path. And there will often be someone ready to shoot down our ideas. However, it's only by gathering up our courage, taking some risks, and making the inevitable mistakes which accompany them, that we can hope to create something genuinely new and worth while. Why not celebrate anarchy as well as conformity; subversion as well as conventionality?

Being a writer, people sometimes say to me 'I wish I could be creative like you, but I just don't have the imagination.' (The people who say this are inevitably creative in their own lives – they just don't realize it.) As with any creative endeavour, though, there's an awful lot of slog and technique involved in what I do, and often only tiny sparks of imagination. I'd like to adapt a quote that I use later on in this book, which sums up the creative, and writing, process perfectly: 'Being a writer is 1 per cent inspiration and 99 per cent perspiration.' So, as well as encouraging our children to apply creativity to every area of their lives, and to be brave enough to take plenty of risks, we also have to help them with the 'technique' part of the process. We must encourage and support them through the 99 per cent of tough slog involved in the creativity equation.

Finally, I'd like to comment briefly on the title of this book, and outline my own creative processes in so doing. Obviously, it's part of what has become known as 'the Buggers series' – an entity that seems increasingly to have grown bigger than any single one of the books. Predictably there have been complaints, although the vast majority of reaction has been overwhelmingly positive. To my detractors I would like to say that, despite being tempted on occasions, I have not spent my entire teaching career using bad language in my classroom, and that I do not advocate calling children 'buggers' while they're actually in the room. Having said that, the title of these books is designed to acknowledge that sometimes, just sometimes, we do get understandably frustrated with our students. To my mind, 'buggers' has always been used in my books in an affectionate rather than a pejorative sense, in the same way that I think of my ex-students as 'kids' rather than the more formal 'pupils'.

Up until the last couple of weeks before completion, this book was going to be called *Getting the Buggers to be Creative*. As I was writing, though, this title began to trouble me more and more. I was struck by an image of teachers cracking the whip in their classrooms, and saying 'come on you little ******s (fill in the blanks to your own satisfaction), be creative or else.' Of course, this rather goes against the nature of what creativity is all about. We can't *force* our children into being creative; it's more about finding ways to harness a talent that they already have.

I did briefly consider whether I could call the book *Getting the Gubbers to be Creative*, before throwing that idea out on the grounds that it was just a touch too bizarre for public consumption. The idea of a play on words appealed, though, so I tucked it in the back of my mind and continued to write. The next stage in my thinking was to wonder whether I should actually go for an entirely different title. Something wet like *Developing a Creative Classroom*, or some such. But it just didn't feel right.

With no alternative title in sight, I decided to stick with what I had: it was the best fit that I could find, and it would just have to do. Then last night I had one of those wonderful 'eureka moments'. The answer dropped into my brain with absolutely no effort at all, a bit like the final piece of a jigsaw slipping into place. So, I give you *Letting the Buggers be Creative* – and I hope that's exactly what this book will help you do.

Sue Cowley
www.suecowley.co.uk

1 Creativity: what's it all about?

It is better to have enough ideas for some of them to be wrong, than to be always right by having no ideas at all.

Edward de Bono

Before we can even start to encourage our children to be more creative, it stands to reason that we need to have a reasonably clear idea of what creativity involves. In this chapter I give an introduction to the subject of creativity – an overview of the subject and its relationship to the work we do as teachers. I look at what creativity actually is, and where it comes from. I explore the reasons why creativity is important, both inside the classroom and in the world beyond the school gates. I also examine the various factors that might get in the way of creativity, and how we can help our students overcome these barriers. Finally, I look at the tricky notion of how we go about assessing creativity.

What is creativity?

A hunch is creativity trying to tell you something.

Frank Capra

During the process of writing this book, I've looked at many different sources to try and pin down a definition for creativity: an answer to the 'what is?' question posed above. Although all these sources find plenty of similarities in the act of creativity, it seems that coming up with a single, definitive definition of this term has proved tricky. Creativity obviously means slightly different things to different people. The sources that I've looked at seem to agree on various key words, including:

- imaginative

- original
- new
- of value
- purposeful.

I'd like to propose that creativity is as much about an attitude as any specific activity – about a process as well as a product. As I pointed out in the Introduction, if we are able to get into a creative frame of mind, we should be able to apply our creativity to pretty much every aspect of our lives. We can approach some of the most mundane of tasks in a creative way, and improve our world in some small way by so doing. Although some activities will clearly involve higher levels of creativity than others (painting a picture as opposed to painting a wall), pretty much anything you might care to name can be approached with a sense of creativity. I discuss this 'creative frame of mind' in further detail in Chapter 3 ('The creative child', see pp. 46–8).

Creativity will involve taking imaginative and innovative approaches to whatever we do – seeing pretty much anything and everything as a chance to shape something that did not exist before, with (not intending to sound too highbrow) the hope of advancing the sum total of human existence. If our aim is to develop creativity within schools, it is this attitude of creativity that we need to engender, whatever the subject or skill in question.

It is tempting to believe that creativity is only necessary or applicable in relation to arts subjects, particularly the performing arts. Clearly, drama, dance, art and music will be areas where creativity is key to success, and the same will apply to creative writing, whether poetry or fiction. However, we can just as valuably use our creativity in approaching those subjects outside what is traditionally viewed as being specifically creative. Our learning in science, maths, history, geography, and so on, will also benefit from creative activities and approaches, and from both teacher and students getting into a creative frame of mind.

The divide between the supposedly more creative arts and the more logic-based science subjects is very much a historical, rather than a natural, one. The 'Enlightenment' was a philosophical movement that sought to emphasize the importance of science, with reasoning and rational thinking being key. The 'Romantic' movement which followed among artists and writers was in part a reaction against this, and emphasized the need for feelings and intuition. The way that subjects are typically divided up in our schools can often be a source of problems when it comes to the development of creativity. There are so many cross-curricular links inherent in the creative process: connections between maths and music, for instance, or between history and drama. By dividing the subjects out, particularly at secondary level, we inevitably stifle at least some of the chances for creativity that might otherwise occur.

Some of the material that I've read in the course of writing this book places a strong emphasis on the production of 'an end product' which has some kind of 'value'. Of course, many creative endeavours do culminate in a wonderful and valuable result – the paintings of Monet or the music of Bach. But this is not to say that we cannot be creative without ever ending up with any one specific end result. Sometimes we will apply our creativity to an idea or a problem, but an outcome that has 'value' will elude us. We might end up with a result that we don't like, or that doesn't seem worth the attention of a wider audience. At this point we will need to ask ourselves the 'chuck or keep?' question that I discuss in Chapter 2 (see pp. 36–7).

I rather suspect that this desire for a worthwhile finished outcome is a result of the way that our educational system is organized. The emphasis is on having something to 'prove' that creativity has been undertaken, and also an end product which can be judged or assessed against other children and other schools. I deal with the thorny area of assessing creativity at the end of this chapter, and look at whether assessment is either appropriate or necessary when viewed in relation to creative endeavours.

Creativity is clearly a complex beast, but at heart it can be broken down into two basic stages. The first step in behaving creatively is to find and work with an initial idea or impulse, playing around with the thoughts that we produce and sometimes searching for other material to develop our thinking. The second step is the process of putting order onto those initial ideas, with the hope and intention of producing some kind of end product (although, as I mentioned above, this will not necessarily be achieved). Of course, these two stages will overlap and vary according to the task at hand and the person or people undertaking it. For a far more detailed explanation of the creative process, see Chapter 2.

It is the nature of the beast that the most original, new and creative ideas can seem a little crazy at first. When being creative, we are constantly pushing at the limits of what is acceptable. During his lifetime Van Gogh was viewed with disdain; now, his paintings are seen as some of the finest examples of art ever produced. If 'value' is indeed what we are after from our creative endeavours, then the price tags attached to Van Gogh's paintings would seem to underline their worth. The issue of creative endeavours being ahead of their time applies equally to the work of modern-day artists and those working creatively in other fields – consider, for instance, the scorn with which many traditionalists view conceptual art. The creative person is inevitably going to be 'out on a limb', because he or she will be suggesting or using original and innovative ideas.

There is nothing neat or tidy about creativity, at least not in the myriad steps leading up to the 'end product' (if one is produced). The willingness to take risks and to get it wrong plays a really key part in the ability to be creative. Creativity usually starts out with an explosion of ideas onto which some kind of form will eventually be put. The quote from Edward de Bono at the start of this chapter sums this up – we need lots of these ideas, no matter whether some of them are 'wrong', do not end up working for us, or perhaps take us down a cul-de-sac. The ability to put a structure on this initial explosion of ideas is a key part of being creative – technique must sit alongside inspiration and innovation if what we produce is to be more than just an explosion of ideas.

It is sometimes said that there is nothing new in the world. Certainly, it would be hard for the children we teach to produce ideas that are innovative on a world stage. However, our students will certainly be finding ideas that are new to *them*, new in relation to what they have produced before, or new relative to what others in their peer group might produce.

Finally, in this brief overview of some of the key attributes of creativity, it's important to remember that creativity is not solely an individual pursuit. The creative endeavour can just as fruitfully be a group event as a solo one. The teacher working with a class might organize small groups into working together on a single creative task, or separately so that each group pursues a creative direction of its own. In my experience, there is also a special kind of power when the class works together as one unit. These whole-class creative endeavours can, of course, produce wonderful outcomes. But they can do much more than this – they can also help us develop strong bonds between our children, uniting the group as they undertake a creative endeavour together.

Where does creativity come from?

When I am in my painting, I'm not aware of what I'm doing. The painting has a life of its own. I try to let it come through.

Jackson Pollock

Historically, the creative impulse has been closely linked to notions of spirituality. Even the most hardened atheist will probably be able to understand this – the feeling that creative ideas are coming from somewhere or something 'outside' of ourselves. The link is even there in the words that we use – 'creativity' being a close relative of the word 'creator'. At the highest levels of creative endeavour music, science, art, fiction, and so on can help to articulate our deepest feelings – to explain the inexplicable. Creativity can be the bolt of lightning which apparently comes out of nowhere, and lets us open, for a moment, what the writer Aldous Huxley called the 'doors of perception'.

Creativity will inevitably come about as a combination of previous experiences – as a kind of accumulation of everything that you have done and encountered in your life. The work that I do now as a writer and teacher is not a separate entity from my earliest career as a dancer, and from the music and art which surrounded me in my youth. Dance, art, music and books all feed into every creative piece on which I spend time and, indeed, into my work as a teacher as well. Although I would often be hard put to specify exactly how and where they are influencing my creativity, I can certainly vouch that they do so in some subconscious and indefinable way. I suspect that a sense of movement plays a key part – those aspects of flow, pace, rhythm and space which are so integral to dance feeding into the way in which I write and teach.

On the other hand, it is sometimes not entirely obvious where that creative spark comes from – it can seem to materialize out of nothing. Speaking from my own perspective as a writer, there are moments when the ideas just flood into my brain. This flow of thoughts will often happen at the most unexpected (and indeed awkward) times. At these moments, I grab whatever scrap of paper is at hand and scribble down the ideas so that I don't lose them. Some writers and artists will have a working notebook that comes with them everywhere they go – a place to note down these ideas before they are lost forever. You could instigate something similar in your classroom – a kind of rough book in which the children can scribble down thoughts, ideas, images, that could potentially be used in a creative piece of work.

You might have heard some artists talk about how they feel that they are simply giving shape or form to something that already seems to exist – a feeling summarized by the Jackson Pollock quote at the start of this section. Sculptors sometimes talk about 'freeing' the sculpture from a block of stone or a piece of wood, some artists of 'seeing' a picture in the mind's eye before it has even been painted. I have certainly experienced this feeling on occasions. Sometimes, and it doesn't happen often, it can feel almost as though my books write themselves. The ability to plug into this sensation, what might be termed a 'hotline to the muse', is at least partly about achieving total focus and concentration.

Of course, this is all very well, but as teachers we must find realistic ways of sparking that creative impulse within the reality of our classrooms. In this book you will find a myriad of ideas to help you do just that. In brief, though, creative ideas might come from a whole variety of sources:

- Finding a combination of elements – seeing old things in a new way.
- Examining the relationships between different things or ideas.
- Responding to a specific stimulus.
- Taking the germ of an idea and letting it bubble.
- Being completely and wildly experimental.
- The 'spark' of inspiration that cannot be explained.

Why is creativity important?

When an aspect of education becomes 'trendy' (learning styles, thinking skills, and now creativity) it is all too easy to get sucked into 'doing it' just because everyone else says that it is important. If our aim is to increase levels of creativity in our students and our schools, and also in society as a whole, then we need to have a clear understanding about why it is actually important to do this. We need to believe that it is worth while. There are many reasons why it might be important to take a creative approach to what we do, and these include the following:

- *It's fun!*: Before I get into some of the more worthy reasons why creativity is a good thing, perhaps the most important reason of all is the simplest: being creative can be a huge amount of fun! Getting some paint out and making a mess as you try to paint a picture; putting some music on and letting your body bend and stretch to the beat; singing at the top of your voice in the shower. And in a school system where we are often plagued by our children's disaffection and a lack of engagement, surely letting them have a bit of fun is a really, really good idea.

- *Advancing humanity*: At its highest and most innovative levels, creativity can and has led to advances in all different areas of human existence. From the great breakthroughs of the scientific world, to the most aesthetically delightful paintings of the great artists. The students we teach might not yet be working at the level of the creative genius. Right at this moment, though, there are children sitting in classrooms who will advance humanity during their lifetimes. How wonderful to be even partially responsible for lighting the spark of creativity in their minds.

- *An impact on our world*: In a world that seems to become ever more complex and diverse, we can be left feeling a bit set adrift from society. The ability to be creative gives us at least some feeling that we can impact on, make sense of, or better, the world in which we live. That we can, in some small way, make a contribution.

- *A cultural expression*: Creativity is very much a part of our own cultural experiences. We inevitably express ourselves in a way that is deeply rooted in the culture from which we come, and in doing so we become part of an ongoing tradition. We can also strengthen our bonds and links with the community in which we live, through expressing our own creative impulses. In a multicultural society, cultures will inevitably mix and intermingle (not always successfully). Creativity offers a way of finding positive links and connections between the different cultures that exist side by side in our society.

- *A sense of unity*: I talk further on in this book about creativity as a group event (see pp. 39–43). When we do create something together with others, this provides a unique kind of bond between us. Some creative endeavours are only made possible through the teamwork that occurs in many schools (I'm thinking particularly of school productions, in which diverse people come together to make the end result possible).

- *Enriching our lives*: The ability to be creative can enhance our lives in many ways: creativity is important for what it offers us as human beings. It is practically impossible to imagine a world without art, music and books. Our lives would be far poorer if it were not for the aesthetic and personal pleasure that the creative impulse can provide.

- *Personal fulfilment*: Creativity can give us a sense of personal fulfilment – both with the 'end product', such as a beautiful watercolour, and also by simply being involved with the creative process. It helps us feel good about ourselves. This sense of creative fulfilment is in stark contrast to the destructive impulses that can arise when a child has a low sense of self-esteem.

- *Success for our society*: A society where skills are highly valued will certainly be good at manufacturing and making things. However, it is the society that values and develops creativity that will be able to invent new things, take new approaches, have new ideas. This is the type of society that will be truly successful in our rapidly changing world.

- *Change and adaptation*: We live in an ever changing world, in which we must develop the ability to adapt to rapidly changing circumstances. This might mean learning to use new technologies; it could also involve adapting to different careers or jobs during our lives. Creativity helps us find ways of adapting and developing to suit our changing circumstances.

• *Improved self-esteem*: Creating something beautiful or worth while can give people a tremendous sense of achievement – the 'I did that!' feeling. It can improve our children's self-esteem no end, helping to develop and sustain their motivation both within and beyond school.

• *Discovering our own strengths*: 'Achievement' is not just about academic ability. Harnessing the individual's creativity gives each child the chance to discover his or her own strengths and abilities. For those children who find the more academic subjects a struggle, discovering an innate sense of creativity can make a real difference in maintaining engagement at school.

• *Problem solving*: Creativity is a great aid in many aspects of problem solving. With a creative frame of mind, we can find ways of solving the problems we already face, but we can also search for those problems which have not yet become apparent. A creative frame of mind will help us search for and evaluate a whole range of alternative solutions.

What gets in the way of creativity?

In schools, and in 'real life' as well, there are many barriers put in the way of the creative impulse. These barriers are built both within ourselves and also as a result of various external factors and pressures. Some of the things that get in the way of creativity will include:

• *'I'm not creative'*: The feeling or conviction that you lack creativity will inevitably get in the way of actually creating something. This feeling might come about because of a lack of confidence – perhaps that person has been put down or criticized in the past when he or she tried to create something. This feeling can also come about when we are not being given the intellectual tools and approaches that are needed for making sense of our creative urges.

• *Fear of risk taking*: Many of us do fear the risk taking (and, indeed, mistake making) that is such an integral part of being creative. As soon as we put something of our own out into the world, there will always be the risk that people might criticize or deride what we have done. With creativity, the person involved will often become incredibly close to the 'thing' that he or she has created. Any criticism can consequently be particularly hurtful if it is not constructive. (Of course, those who are creative for a living must accept this as a necessary evil.) We do seem to have evolved a school system that views mistakes as an enemy to be feared and avoided. Unless we can allow an element of risk and error into our children's education, creativity will remain a distant dream.

- *Familiar associations*: If we are to shape something that is genuinely new or innovative, we need to be able to shrug off any familiar associations and come up with ideas of our own. This can be a particular problem for children, who will often lack the experiences of the world that feed into the creative process. For instance, when doing improvisations in my drama lessons, I sometimes find that children produce a scene replicated from the television. They go with what is familiar and known, rather than taking the risk of improvising their way to something new.

- *Trying to create an 'end product' in one*: We are sometimes guilty of expecting our children to move straight on to producing a finished piece of work. This is entirely understandable when we are under the pressures of time, the constraints of the curriculum, the feeling that we need to have something to 'show' for any class time that we spend. Unfortunately, this approach can lead to some children feeling that they are not creative because they find it impossible to jump straight to a completed piece of work.

- *Lack of experience*: Those involved in creativity will always, whether consciously or subconsciously, be drawing on their own previous experiences, and also on the traditions of those who have been creative in the past. In many ways, when being creative, we are always walking in the footsteps of those who have gone before. This is particularly so when it comes to the great creative innovators of art, literature, science, and so on. We need to expose our students to the creative efforts of those who have gone before, to develop a backdrop of experience which informs their own work.

- *Lack of technique*: It is also the case that children will typically not have sufficient experience or knowledge of the relevant techniques and structures used in the different subject areas. Transmitting these techniques is, of course, a key part of what we as teachers do. A person can have all the innovative ideas in the world but, without being able to give these ideas form and structure, he or she will be unable to communicate what is meant to an audience.
- *Over-reliance on techniques*: Of course, there will also be times when an over-reliance on the techniques of a subject will stifle creativity. We can get so wrapped up in technical accuracy that we develop an unhealthy fear of breaking the rules. Sometimes techniques must be learned in order to have the courage to discount them or throw them away. Some of the great creative works of history would be unlikely to pass muster in a SATs or GCSE exam (James Joyce's *Ulysses*, for example).
- *Lack of time*: From the school's or the teacher's perspective, there is often very little free time within the daily timetable. This is a big problem when it comes to creativity. We often cannot (or are not allowed to) find or put aside the amount of time needed for our children to play around with their ideas. If this remains the case, then there is very little chance of us encouraging true creativity within our education system.
- *'My subject isn't creative'*: Sometimes the problems will come from the attitudes or assumptions of the teacher. An expectation that a particular curriculum area is not creative will often arise from the unnatural divisions between subjects in our schools. If the teacher cannot see the value of creativity within a subject, despite all those dreaded curriculum demands, then he or she will inevitably teach in a way that values skills and techniques over innovation.

Overcoming the barriers to creativity

Having established the various factors that can get in the way of creativity, our next step as teachers will naturally be to try and overcome these problems. That way we can have some hope of encouraging our children to be genuinely creative. Of course, many (perhaps most) children seem to be naturally motivated to create something of their own. This gift can, however, be quickly dampened by their upbringing and by the education system in which they find themselves. It strikes me that the disaffection and misbehaviour that many teachers face in the classroom is caused, at least in part, by the lack of creativity in our schools.

Here, then, is some practical advice about ways in which you can help your children jump the hurdles that stand in their way.

- *We are all creative*: Make it clear to your students that they all have it within them to be creative people. Search for and acknowledge every child's creativity, whatever shape or form it takes. Keep an ever watchful eye out for any examples of the creative in your classroom, aiming to do so particularly for those children who struggle to achieve in an academic setting. When you do spot even the briefest glimpse of creativity, acknowledge and praise it in a way that works for you. This is not to say you should praise anything and everything – for it to have value, your acknowledgement must be honest and genuine. To give an example, a child with poor literacy skills might present his teacher with a pretty dreadful attempt at a poem about aeroplanes. However, it could be that he has been creative in the way the poem is presented, writing in diagonal lines at an angle across the page to suggest the plane taking off, and cutting the paper into the shape of a cloud. In this situation, the teacher might praise his imaginative and original presentation skills.
- *Encourage risk taking*: This is very hard to do, and will take courage both from your students and from you as their teacher. We live in a society that feels risk can and should be 'managed'. An unhealthy fear of litigation means that teachers are increasingly discouraged from taking even calculated risks in their work. If we hope to encourage our children to be creative, both they and we absolutely must feel free to make mistakes and take risks with our thinking and our work. Clearly, I'm not suggesting that we throw caution completely to the wind, but we do need to fight against the insidious nature of all that 'risk management' which is pressed upon us. After all, if we never take risks, then we fail to learn the

important lessons of commonsense. Make your students feel that it is acceptable and admirable to take risks when approaching a task, by articulating this to them at every opportunity. Praise those students who have been willing to go out on a limb, even if the end result is not a success. Take risks yourself as well, putting yourself on the line to show the children that you 'walk the walk' as well as talking the talk. Sometimes your attempts will fail, but this is a vital part of the learning process in becoming a more creative person.

- *Encourage innovation*: Aim to pull your children away from simply replicating the creative endeavours of other people. Look for, and praise, those who attempt to shape something that is genuinely new. This might involve a change in your mindset, as you move away from looking for that beautifully finished end product, to hunting down and seeing value in examples of what is original or unique. I'd like to give an example of this from my own practice to illustrate how easy it is to get trapped into searching only for what 'looks good'. I often do work in drama lessons on the crime genre. One part of the work is to produce a scene in which a crime is committed. When these scenes are shown to the class, some children will produce an apparently polished performance, but one which bears a striking resemblance to the previous night's episode of *The Bill*. I have often been tempted to praise these polished scenes over the more innovative, but less well-structured, work of other groups. I have to constantly remind myself that those who do not base their work on something they have already seen are in fact showing far more creativity.

- *Make time for the steps*: Every creative journey will involve our children taking many steps before they get to that 'end product'. We need to make time for this part of the journey, perhaps devoting several lessons to all the messy in between stuff before the finished version is produced. We can help our children during the journey by articulating the possible path that they might tread.

- *Provide access to experience*: We can help to provide the experience that our children might lack – to offer them access to the creative endeavours of those who have walked before them. This is perhaps particularly important for those children who are not given access to books, or art, or music, in their home lives. It might mean sharing examples of great artworks from the distant, and not so distant, past; it could involve sharing with them some of the great scientific discoveries of the past. It might also mean sharing some more everyday experiences with them, for instance by offering them inspirational resources or stimulating activities, such as a visit to a museum. As well as showing them the end results of other people's creativity, it can also be an excellent idea to show them the steps that were taken to get to this point. For instance, examining the working drawings of Leonardo da Vinci, or discussing where the inspiration came from for Newton's discovery of gravity (and perhaps even experiencing that 'eureka moment' by dropping their own apples from the classroom windows).

- *Take advantage of lack of experience*: Conversely, our children's lack of experience can sometimes be a great advantage in harnessing their creativity. Their relative inexperience of the world means that our students have less sense of what 'should be'. In fact, some of the great artists of the twentieth century put aside their technical knowledge and ability to take that step backwards to a more childlike sensibility. Pablo Picasso summed this idea up when he said: 'Every child is an artist. The problem is how to remain an artist once he grows up.'

- *Teach the techniques*: Obviously, each individual teacher will also need to equip his or her children with the techniques that relate to the subject or subjects in question. This part of the creativity equation is typically given plenty of focus and time in our schools. Do take the time to articulate for your class why technique is actually important in the creative process. Take your children by the hand as you show them how to apply form and structure to that initial explosion of ideas.

- *Encourage rule breaking*: Try to be a bit subversive at times – it's not only fun, but it's also a key part of pretty much any creative endeavour. Show your children how and when it is appropriate to break the rules. Refuse to let concerns about exam results turn you into a DfES version of a 'Stepford Teacher'!

- *Rediscover your inner child*: Putting it like that might make me sound like I regularly hug trees, but what I mean is to remember what it was like to discover something for the first time. Step back for a moment from your position as an authority on your subject, and try to approach it from the perspective of a child learning about the wonders of life afresh. You might know how to work out the angle of a triangle (don't ask me, I'm hopeless at maths), but you would hopefully be able to help your children take a creative path to discover this for themselves.

Assessing creativity

> I have spread my dreams under your feet;
> Tread softly because you tread on my dreams.
> *W. B. Yeats*

Creativity takes courage: bravery is involved every time we bring something of our own into being. The question, 'What will other people think or say about this?' is never far from our minds. Risk taking forms an integral part of each creative endeavour: we effectively put ourselves on the line during the act of creation. The very youngest children perhaps feel this pressure the least – they have not yet gained the sense that other people might have an opinion or be critical about what they do. As soon as this concept of judgement arrives, creativity can start to feel like a very scary thing to do. There is a real fragility involved in being creative – the urge or impulse to create is easily damaged or broken.

In many ways, much of the formal assessment we do is the complete antithesis of creativity. It mitigates against creativity because it asks the student 'what's the right answer?', rather than 'what possible answers might there be?' I would like to outline here some of the reasons why I believe that the assessment of creativity should be approached (if at all) with the very greatest of care.

- *The concept of 'value'*: The word 'value' is over-used in the educational world. It is as though education has become a supermarket, in which every product (a piece of work, an individual student, a school) must be judged for its worth in relation to a set of 'standards', and then compared to the worth of others. But in schools, and in education generally, value can be very much a relative concept. Consider that scrappy piece of paper, handed to you by a child who is functionally illiterate. It has three lines of poetry on it that must have taken genuine effort and commitment and, despite the poor presentation, the ideas are interesting and imaginative. Now look at that three-page epic poem dashed off by a child who finds English easy. It is beautifully presented, and at first sight appears far more polished and creative. But which of these pieces of work has more 'value' to the individual concerned and to the teacher reading it? And which child is most likely to be de-motivated by critical judgements?

- *The dangers of de-motivation:* The moment we start to judge what our children produce, we are in danger of scaring them away from their creative endeavours. When we assess our children's work, we are effectively saying what is right or wrong, good or bad, about it. Creativity, on the other hand, is about freedom of expression, about finding a unique way of expressing ourselves, preferably without any fear of making mistakes. Many of the children that we teach are sufficiently stressed and de-motivated, without us adding further to their load by assessing their efforts at creativity.

- *The role of the teacher:* I'm not entirely convinced that we as teachers have any right to judge the 'value' of what our children produce when they are engaged in such a nebulous process as that of being creative. I also worry that assessing creative pieces is likely to damage the often fragile relationship that we have with our students. If we ask our children to put themselves on the line, by presenting us with work that is uniquely theirs, then they must trust us not to squash their efforts underfoot.

- *The subjective observer:* Judging one piece of creativity against another is often a pretty meaningless exercise, one in which the particular likes, dislikes and opinions of the observer cannot be factored out of the equation. Who would dare to say whether *To Kill a Mockingbird* is a 'better' book than *Catcher in the Rye*? Whether da Vinci's *Mona Lisa* is a 'greater' piece of art than Constable's *The Haywain*? Or whether Newton's discovery of gravity was a more fundamental and important scientific development than Galileo's contention that the Earth revolves around the sun? Similarly, judging creativity in one medium (say, painting) against that in another (say, sculpture) is problematic to say the least. These difficulties are only magnified once we try to judge creativity across the barriers of different subject areas.

- *The values of society*: The creative worth of what we produce is not necessarily recognized at the time. Van Gogh died in poverty, his creative genius completely ignored, whereas today his paintings fetch millions. Creative people are typically ahead of their time, and may well outreach that which society currently views as 'of value'. That bizarre idea proposed by your Year 10 physics student might seem worthless right now, but in ten years' time could prove to be part of the answer to one of the great puzzles of science.

- *The build-up of appreciation*: Similarly, some creative pieces take a while to appreciate. You may have experienced this with music: the first time you hear a song on the radio you can't see what all the fuss is about. But with repeated listenings it grabs you more and more, until you begin to feel that it's a great song. In an artwork that has many layers of meaning, our first impressions might simply deal with the surface value. However, the more we look at and the deeper we look into it, the more we appreciate the achievement of the artist, and the more pleasure we can gain.

- *The role of the audience*: On a wider scale, any creative piece which is sent out into the world is eventually going to be judged, not by one single assessor at one single moment in time, but by the wider audience for which it is intended. How 'good' a creative piece is must surely be at least partially about how many people it touches, or delights, or changes in some way. 'Word of mouth' plays a powerful part in the success of many creative endeavours – when enough people start saying 'this is good, you should look at it', a kind of momentum develops. For instance, the huge success Lynne Truss's *Eats, Shoots & Leaves* offers a great example of the power of word of mouth.

- *The 'chuck or keep?' decision*: If we are to undertake assessment, we are obviously assuming that there will be an 'end product' worthy of actually keeping. Depending on the creative person's levels of perfectionism, there will be some (perhaps many) times when the finished result does not live up to expectations. It is an integral part of the creative journey that, if we feel we have not reached the destination that we intended, or if we do not believe the end point of the journey is the 'right' one, we are free and able to throw the finished result away. For more thoughts on this, see 'The "chuck or keep?" question' in Chapter 2, pp. 36–7.

- *What's the point?*: Finally, I do wonder what the *point* actually is of assessing our students' levels of creativity? If our intention is to enhance the creativity of each individual, then what does it actually serve us to have a way of comparing one child against another? Can we help Child A become more creative by judging her work against that of Child B; will we assist School X in becoming a more creative place by analysing its achievements against School Y? And if not, is there really any point in taking the risk of damaging the self-esteem and motivation of children, teachers and schools?

Although there will typically be some technique involved in any creative effort, the true worth of an innovative piece will be in the responses that it evokes in a wider sense. When responding to examples of creativity, we might ask ourselves:

- Does it move me?
- Does it send a shiver down my spine?
- Does it delight me?
- Does it touch me?
- Does it help me?
- Is it beautiful?
- Is it meaningful?
- Do I enjoy it?
- Would I like to read/see/hear/watch/use it again?
- Do I feel a deep need to read/see/hear/watch/use it again?
- Does it enhance my understanding of the world?
- Does it help me see something in a new light?
- Does it alter my perceptions of the world?
- Does it make me laugh/smile/cry?
- Has it changed my life?

With the questions above in mind, I'd like to end this chapter with a final, rather cheeky, thought on assessing creativity. I do hope you enjoy this extract from a (purely fictional, I hasten to add) DfES directive:

Assessing creativity

Teachers should judge a pupil's levels of creativity with reference to the following assessment criteria.

1. *Does it move me?*

Tick the relevant box on the scale given from 1 to 5, with 1 being 'it doesn't move me at all' and 5 being 'it moves me deeply'.

2. *Does it send a shiver down my spine?*

On the scale provided, estimate the length of the shiver provided by the work. If no shiver was discerned, tick the 'failure to create shiver' box.

2 The creative journey

Two roads diverged in a wood, and I –
I took the one less travelled by
And that has made all the difference.
Robert Frost

This chapter examines the various stages involved in the creative process: what I've called the 'creative journey'. As teachers, we need to understand the various stages of this journey so that we can encourage our students to demonstrate and develop their own creativity. Seeing the journey laid bare should help us move away from imagining that an 'end product' can somehow miraculously be produced, without much effort or time being involved. It will also enable us to guide our children as they set off on their own journeys of creative discovery.

In this chapter I look first at whether the creative process can actually be taught, and at how we might go about teaching it. I also examine the balance between the extremes of freedom and control that must exist simultaneously during every journey of creativity. I take a brief look at the different forms in which we might express ourselves, and at the impact which the choice of form will have on the creative process. I then examine in detail the various different stages that might be undertaken during a creative journey. Finally, I look at how we can help our students undertake their creative endeavours in group settings.

Can the creative process be taught?

In brief, of course it can! Every person has it within themselves to be creative, and we as teachers can play a key part in helping our students map out their own individual journeys. Some of the children we teach might not have been given the early experiences that help us to develop a creative frame of mind. However, we as teachers can certainly play a game of 'catch up' in providing these experiences, and nurture the seeds of creativity that lie dormant in our children's minds.

All the children that we teach will have their own individual strengths, and this includes the forms which their individual creativity takes. Whether these are to do with nature or nurture is really neither here nor there – as teachers, we can only work with the raw material that we have. Our role is to develop each child's learning in all subject areas in the best way that we possibly can, and this includes his or her creative potential.

Some children might find that their talents lie specifically in art, or dance, or music, or maths; others will have a wider range of creative potential. And it's this potential that we need to nurture and develop. We might feel that some children have more latent creativity in some subjects than in others, although I would argue that all children are potentially creative in all the school subjects and beyond. Our aim as teachers should be to encourage every individual child to approach any area of the curriculum with the creative frame of mind discussed in the first chapter of this book.

It is often assumed that the 'creative genius' does not have to put much effort into his or her work: that the first step described below, that of inspiration, is enough to sweep the person towards a miraculously creative end result. While this might be the case in a tiny minority of situations, in most instances there will be a lengthy and tough journey to undertake. In many instances, the initial spark of inspiration, or the later 'shaft of light' (see below) will represent only a tiny part of the total time spent on the creative process. It is the perspiration of playing with and shaping our ideas, and the investigation stage in which we look for further information or background, that often make up the largest part of a creative journey.

As teachers, we have various opportunities when it comes to encouraging or teaching our students to be more creative. These are dealt with in lots of detail throughout this book, but in brief we will be:

- Helping them find sources of inspiration – whether providing these for the class, or encouraging our children to seek out their own.

- Encouraging them to play around with the ideas that they develop, by creating a climate that nurtures rather than damages their inherent motivation to be creative.
- Providing them with experiences that contribute to, or inspire, their creative impulses, whatever the subject being taught.
- Providing information and ideas about the relevant techniques and structures that will lend shape and form to the work.
- Offering an environment in which creativity seems natural, comfortable and worth while.
- Showing our students how to reflect on and review the outcomes of the creative process.

Finding a balance

At all times during the process of creativity, there will be an intricate balance between abandon and restraint, between freedom and control. An explosion of untamed ideas is all very well, but for these ideas to make any sense or to convey what is intended to an audience, a certain level of control must be achieved. Unfortunately, the tendency in our education system has been to emphasize structure and control at the cost of freedom and abandon. Any loss of control has been criticized and seen as evidence that teachers 'do not care' about technique (the classic accusations about teachers who just let their children 'play around' without teaching them skills and techniques). As teachers, we must find a way through this maze – a way of helping our children achieve a balance in their creative work.

In some cases, this balance will tip more towards freedom and loss of control – letting chance and the accidental play an integral part in giving shape to the work, as in the 'drip and splash' paintings of the artist Jackson Pollock. In other instances, a far tighter rein will be kept on the whole experience. In the majority of situations, a subtle balance between the two impulses will be integral to the end creative result.

Schools are not necessarily the best places to nurture the freedom and abandon part of the creative equation. The problem is that big organizations such as schools do have to impose at least some sense of order and structure if things are not going to very quickly fall apart. The demands of the curriculum – the sense that we must 'get through it all' – and the very nature of the school day trap us into a position where we often have little time to allow our children to be creative. The pressure to have something concrete (that 'end product') to assess or examine can also present problems. How can we allow our children the freedom to make mistakes and to throw these away, if the emphasis is on having something to assess?

Nevertheless, the best teachers are willing to let a little bit of chaos into their classrooms – to take those risks that are such a central part of creativity. It is our job to find ways of balancing that chaos and freedom with structure and control as required. As well as there being a balance between freedom and control in the children's creative work, the teacher will also need to teach in a way that balances these two opposing forces. This is a tricky balance to achieve, and one which I discuss in some detail in Chapter 4 (see pp. 69–77).

A thought about form

The form into which any creative endeavour is being shaped will play a powerful part in deciding how the journey is going to progress. This is apparent if you examine the forms used in different subjects (the novel versus the song), but it will also apply in forms being used within the same subject area (the novel versus the poem). A three-minute pop song clearly has a radically different form to an hour-long symphony; similarly, a full-length novel obviously presents a very different form to a haiku. While the overall creative journey will remain pretty much the same, the ways in which the various stages are used will inevitably differ.

Where the form is relatively short (the poem, the pop song), the quality of what the piece encapsulates will be that much more vital. In these cases, much of what the creative person does will involve applying the 'chuck or keep?' question described below (see pp. 36–7). On occasions, the songwriter might be able to walk straight through the process and end up with a brilliant end product. But for every example of this, there will also be those instances where fifty different versions are rejected before a final result is reached.

The journey

It is good to have an end to journey toward; but it is the journey that matters, in the end.

Ursula K. Le Guin

In this section I'm going to offer you a rough overview of the various steps involved in the creative journey. This is not a 'rough' overview in the sense of a draft, but rough because the process is very hard to pin down – it has an inbuilt variability, an inherent slipperiness. The steps and stages involved will differ widely according to:

- the subject or subjects involved (art or music, science or maths, etc.)
- the medium being used (words or numbers, images or sounds, etc.)
- the person or people involved (personality, motivations, experiences, etc.)
- the culture or society within which we are working
- the specifics of what is actually being created – the form of the piece
- the likely audience for or recipient of the end product (if one is produced).

One of the key points to remember is that the stages outlined below will not necessarily come in any exact order. The person or persons involved in the creative process may well jump backwards and forwards between the various steps, attitudes and skills involved during the course of the creative journey.

Inspiration

Inspiration can mean many different things, and different people will find inspiration in completely different ways. Inspiration will often provide us with an excellent 'starting point' for our creative endeavours, but it can also play a part once we have actually begun to work. Inspiration acts as a stimulus to the creative parts of our minds. This part of the process is probably best described by using a metaphor. If undertaking the creative journey is driving a car, then the inspiration stage is the act of turning the key to start up the engine. It is that initial spark which allows the engine to fire up, before the driver puts his or her car into gear and pulls out into the road.

During the creative journey, there will often be occasions when the car engine stalls, and the driver needs to restart the engine before he or she can continue. As I emphasized at the beginning of this section, the various stages will not necessarily come in any one specific order, or we may need to return to the earlier stages several times over. Stalling the car of creativity does not mean that you are a bad driver. Rather, it means that you are coming across the inevitable blind alleys that form an integral part of the creative process – that you are willing to take some risks and make some mistakes if it helps you in reaching a more interesting destination.

As creative people, and as teachers, we can find inspiration from many different sources. To a certain extent this will depend on the subject or topic with which we are working, although there are many instances where inspiration can be an entirely cross-curricular matter. So it is that in English, our inspiration might come from the look, sound or meaning of a word or phrase. However, that same inspiration might be used to spark a picture in art. Similarly, we might use a photograph of a specific location to spark off some creative work in a history lesson, and we might use that same photo to develop our students' creativity in geography.

Working with an inspiration will often be a case of close observation. When we interact at a detailed level with an object, a question, or a piece of music, ideas and potential connections will often be brought to mind. Conversely, working with inspiration can also mean stepping back from the source, to take a wider overview. There is certainly no need to sit around waiting for inspiration to drift down from the sky – once we get going with an initial stimulus we should quickly find ourselves feeling inspired.

Below you will find a list of some potential sources of inspiration. There are lots more ideas in Chapter 5, in the section on 'Finding inspiration' (see pp. 86–8). In fact, I could have filled this entire book with a list of inspirational starting points! The suggestions that you offer to your own students, and indeed the ideas that they themselves present you with, can be as varied and as diverse as you wish. You might be using:

- images
- words
- sounds
- music
- objects
- sensory responses – smells, textures, tastes
- places
- problems
- questions
- imagination.

After that initial burst of inspiration has taken place, your children will move into the improvisational phase of the creative process. However, it is worth bearing in mind that inspiration might be necessary or useful at any point during the journey. For instance, although the creative journey will often be 'kick started' by inspiration, it also plays a key part in the 'shaft of light' described below.

Improvisation
If you want to up your success rate, you need to up your failure rate.

Unknown

During the improvisation phase of the journey, the person or group moves on from that initial spark or idea and into the phase where the piece begins to develop. What I call 'improvisation' is often described as 'play'. It could also usefully (and perhaps more honestly) be entitled 'fiddling around'. At this stage of the process, the person or people involved will be gathering and developing lots of ideas, and starting to shuffle things around to see how they work together. This is where the search for the 'best fit' starts, where the hunt begins to find some kind of shape within the material.

Some of the attitudes and approaches involved in the improvisational phase of creativity include:

- Gathering vast quantities of ideas and impressions, without too much concern about what is 'right' or 'wrong'.
- Arranging and rearranging these ideas to see what might occur.
- Playing around with ideas to see where they lead (this could be described as 'taking an idea for a walk').

- Experimenting – trying various things out (methods, approaches, combinations) to see how they work.
- Questioning – asking what/why/how/when type questions.
- Stretching and developing – taking an idea and seeing how it might be extended.
- Adapting and modifying – changing or rearranging the ideas to look for an internal shape, or to get closer to what is intended.
- Finding connections between various different thoughts – often, the more unusual the connection, the more interesting it will be.
- Drafting and redrafting in a search for an internal shape or in the hope of being struck by the 'shaft of light' (see below).
- Going down dead ends, making lots of mistakes, throwing away (see below, 'The "chuck or keep?" question').

You can't make an omelette without breaking some eggs.

Unknown

During the improvisation stage, it is important to silence the 'internal critic' who metaphorically sits on our shoulders. This is the critic who subconsciously tells us 'you can't do that' or 'that doesn't look very good' or 'that's crazy, no one could possibly believe that.' By silencing the voice of reason, a huge range of ideas can be accumulated and amassed. Many of these ideas might turn out to be worthless, but it is often the thought from far out on left field that actually turns out to be the key to it all. From the point of having millions of ideas, we can always move on to cut away any stuff that doesn't work for us. The ability to silence the fear of what other people will think is crucial in finding new and original ideas.

There are many different ways or styles of improvising. Some of us will prefer a relatively structured approach to this stage, in which we will work simultaneously on the 'shaping' phase described below. Others will prefer to simply 'go with the flow', for instance the crime writer Elmore Leonard, who will take a single character and see where he or she leads.

The shaft of light

Every revolutionary idea seems to evoke three stages of reaction. They may be summed up by the phrases: (1) It's completely impossible. (2) It's possible, but it's not worth doing. (3) I said it was a good idea all along.

Sir Arthur C. Clarke

At certain points during the process of creativity, there may come a breakthrough moment. An answer to what has been puzzling you suddenly occurs. An idea that seems new and radical, but which might just work, comes into your mind. An image encapsulating everything you intended to put across begins to appear. A connection springs into your view that makes sense of everything that has gone before. On these occasions, it is as though something floats into your mind out of nowhere and conveniently provides the solution to what has been puzzling you.

I've used the image of a 'shaft of light' to describe these breakthrough moments, because they are literally like an illumination of something that you've not noticed or seen before. During the creative process there may be several of these shafts of light, or they might not happen at all. In some arenas, the whole creative process might start with the shaft of light – it can provide that initial source of inspiration. This will be particularly so in subject areas where creativity is about finding new ideas or concepts, such as science and maths. A radical idea or thought might hit, and this is then tested to see whether it stands up to closer scrutiny, as in the Arthur C. Clarke quote given above. These breakthrough moments seem to be a case of the brain taking a lateral leap in its thinking.

Of course, entirely original ideas are relatively rare. The shaft of light will not necessarily mean your children finding something that is new *per se*, but rather it could mean realizing something that is new *to them*. It is as though the idea suddenly 'clicks' with the child, and he or she says 'Oh yes, now I see how it works' or 'Aha! That's a good idea.'

There are various circumstances under which the shaft of light seems most likely to hit. I've listed these below, and given some ideas about how you might emulate them in your classroom.

- *Step back*: When working intensively on a creative piece, we can often get so engrossed in the details that we stop seeing the overall picture. At these times, it can prove very useful to step back, or even away, from the piece so that we widen our perspective. Having done this, a new connection or impression might strike us – one that we had not noticed because we were too closely involved.

- *Remove the focus*: When we find ourselves down a cul-de-sac, this can provide the perfect opportunity to take a bit of time away from the creative work. By removing the focus – by taking our minds off the specifics of the problem – an answer will often occur without much effort. Have you ever noticed how, when you are struggling to remember something (a person's name, a specific word), a little while after you have given up searching for it, it suddenly pops into your head? To replicate this in the classroom can be tricky. We can't really let little Jimmy sit at one side of the room while the rest of the class finish off their work. What we can do, though, is accept that some children will need time away from a creative piece before they are able to take it further. For the teacher, this could mean planning for a break in the mid-point of a series of lessons, so that the students can step back from their work and look at it afresh at a later stage.

- *Loosen up*: Historically, some artists have turned to mind-altering substances to help them achieve this moment of illumination. Obviously, I'm not suggesting that you recommend this approach to your children. However, I would be lying if I did not admit that some of my best ideas have come to me with a pen in one hand and a glass of wine in the other! You can certainly help your children loosen up and relax the intensity of their focus by doing some short physical activities, or by taking them into a meditative state (see below for some ideas on how this can be done).

- *Daydreaming*: These breakthroughs will often come in the moments when you first awake, or when you are just drifting off to sleep. The key seems to be shifting your focus away from what has been puzzling you – simply letting the ideas mull themselves over in your mind without any intellectual or rational input. Clearly, the classroom is not really the place for our children to have a nap, although I did once work in an overseas school where the younger students had an afternoon siesta. However, we can certainly use the meditative techniques described below to help simulate this state.

- *Meditations*: Some people use meditations to achieve these moments of illumination: whether the traditional meditation in which you empty your mind of all thoughts, or through simple, repetitive counter-intellectual actions in which you become completely immersed, blocking out conscious thought. Below are a few suggestions for meditative activities that you might like to use in your classroom. You might feel a bit daft at first when suggesting or using these activities, but if you stick with them, and ask your children how they feel about them, you will hopefully be won over. These exercises, and others, are explained in more detail in my book *Getting the Buggers to Think*:

  - *Blue sky*: Ask the children to close their eyes and imagine a clear blue sky, at the same time trying to completely empty their minds of all thoughts. If a thought does come into their heads, they can visualize this as a cloud floating across the sky, and allow it to drift gently away.

  - *Chants*: Choose a word with the children – this should preferably be something calming, like 'soft' or 'clear'. Now get your class to chant the word over and over again to help them clear their minds.

  - *Into the forest*: Ask your students to close their eyes, and then take them for a walk through a 'forest' in their imaginations. Ask a few questions to stimulate their minds and encourage them to use their senses, but avoid giving excessive detail. You can use this exercise with a whole variety of different settings ('on the beach' being a particular favourite with many children).

  - *Repetitive actions*: Any repetitive action that does not require intellectual thought can be used as a meditative exercise. At home, you might do some gardening or DIY to clear your mind of the stresses of the day. In the classroom, you might use repetitive exercises such as colouring in or cutting out.

Investigation
If I have seen further it is by standing on the shoulders of giants.

Sir Isaac Newton

When we set out on a creative journey, we are not the first people ever to travel down that particular road. Every time we apply our creativity, whether this is to an artwork or a scientific theory, we are walking in the footsteps of those who have gone before. These influences might come indirectly – as an ever present background noise that informs the creative piece – or they might come through more specific reference to previous creative works. The 'investigation' that I discuss here might be applied in a literal sense (going to look stuff up), but it might also simply involve a sub-conscious invocation of the creative presence of those who have gone before us.

Depending on the exact nature of the creative endeavour, there will sometimes be a need for a phase in which investigation is undertaken very deliberately. For instance, although this book is essentially a practical one, based on my own experiences, I did spend quite a bit of time reading around the subject before I began to write. It was also necessary to do some further 'investigations' during the stage of actually putting the book together, looking up references and so on. Similarly, a student creating a painting based on the starting point 'water' might start by taking some time to look through images that artists in the past have produced around that same theme. During the course of creating the piece, the child might also decide to spend some time exploring the different properties of water by undertaking some practical experiments.

The investigation part of the process is akin to doing a bit of background research or reading. As with all the other phases of the creative process, investigation will occur as and when it is needed. For the teacher, this is a time where some useful input can be made into the children's work. Indeed, a key part of our role is to provide the students with those prior experiences that play a vital part in creativity. To give an example, if you were creating dances based on the topic of 'animals', you might show the class some video extracts of the ways in which different animals move.

A word of caution needs to be sounded during the investigation stage. When we are looking at material that already exists, it can be incredibly tempting to start nicking bits – whether this means ideas, or even small sections of the work. Of course, what we do will feed out of what has gone before, but creativity means applying our own unique selves to the process. Once we get drawn into simply replicating other people's ideas, we are clearly moving away from what lies at the very heart of creativity. Consequently, when undertaking any investigative activities, it is important to ensure that these only *inform* the creative process. The direction in which our own creative impulses actually take us will still be a case of following our own path.

Shaping
Genius is 1 per cent inspiration, and 99 per cent perspiration.

Thomas Edison

Once at least some of the ideas are in place, the process of shaping the work can begin. However, it is vital to remember that the creative process is not linear. The person involved in being creative might bounce backwards and forwards between each of the phases a number of times before coming to a satisfactory conclusion. The shaping phase of the creative journey is where the majority of the perspiration, as described above by Edison, must be expended.

Shaping a piece will involve making decisions about structure, and it is at this point that technique will begin to play more importance. Clearly, the structures and techniques actually involved in shaping the work will vary widely according to the subject area or areas involved, and also the specifics of what is being created. This is the point at which the ideas have fallen into place, and you are starting to finalize your work for its intended audience. The shaping part of the process can often feel like a bit of a slog. It's great fun having the ideas, but the more technical aspects of putting it all together and finishing it all off can seem a little bit more like hard work. This is the point at which that initial enthusiasm can start to lag.

Once you start to structure the piece, you will often see a need to return to the improvisation stage of the creative process. It could be that the ideas you have don't actually work in the particular way or order that you had at first imagined. It might be that your shaping throws up new ideas and that you need to add some of these in and even throw some of your previous ideas out to make room for them. The ability, and indeed willingness, to bounce backwards and forwards between the various phases is a vital part of the whole creative journey.

Less is often more when it comes to a really beautiful and powerful creative end product. So, during the shaping stage you will also be cutting out the excess from whatever piece it is you are creating. A willingness to throw away material at any point is vital for creativity: we must make hard and sometimes even painful decisions about what simply does not work. We cannot hang onto an idea just because we like it, if it does not work within the context of the creative piece as a whole. In fact, this can even be the case when an 'end product' has been achieved, and the person who has created it decides that it is not fit for public consumption.

To ensure that the process of shaping the work is as successful as possible, there are some factors that the teacher should consider:

- *Entering 'the zone'*: When a piece of creative work is being shaped, the person involved will often seem to move into 'the zone'. This is a place of total concentration, where all external stimuli are blocked out, where nothing except the piece that we are working on seems to exist. Although this sounds like a rather highbrow concept, in fact you may have often noticed how children will go into the zone quite naturally. For instance, a young child might be working so intently on her painting that she does not notice the bell going for lunch. There are a number of mainly environmental factors that can help a person enter the zone. However, it is important for the teacher to realize that individuals will have their own very personal ways of finding a focus. It would be pretty much impossible to sustain the correct conditions for every individual child in your classroom, but it is certainly worth discussing with your class the ways and conditions in which they concentrate and work best. The ability to enter the zone will also depend on the subject involved. For instance, I find it impossible to listen to the radio while writing, because the words get in the way of my writing voice. For someone using a more visual medium, background music might prove very useful. As teachers we can be aware of, and try to overcome,

any factors that might mitigate against our children achieving total focus. These factors will include:
- negative mood
- wrong time of day
- physical condition (tired, hungry)
- lack of space
- environment (messy, overcrowded)
- excessive noise levels.

- *Shape in/shape on?*: It is sometimes the case that we impose a shape on a piece of creative work: we have the ideas, and we simply put them into the best format we can find. Although this is entirely understandable, it is not necessarily the most fruitful approach to take. Instead, encourage your children to look for the shape that lies inside the ideas — allowing the creative piece to grow organically from within.

- *The 'snowball' effect*: There will sometimes come a time towards the end of the shaping process when the work takes on a huge sense of momentum as the person moves towards a finished product. The end is in sight and the piece really begins to take form and shape. If at all possible, we need to let our students take advantage of this momentum when it has built up a head of steam. If the bell goes for lunch, and a child begs you for a further ten minutes to finish her painting because she's 'nearly there', then you might let her snowball continue its descent downhill.

Some thoughts about technique

A key part of our role as teachers is to pass on the techniques of the particular subject area we are teaching, so that our students are free to shape their work in the best way possible. Studying technique can be a fascinating experience, and the self-discipline that this study develops can be a powerful asset to us as individuals. A ballerina might be stretching herself into the splits to help perfect the line of her arabesque; a pianist could be honing his finger movements by practising scales; a mathematician might be sharpening his logic by solving a variety of mathematical problems. However, when it comes to creativity, technique is not an end in itself: it is important only in so far as it frees a person up to express his or her own creative impulses.

Mastering and maintaining technique is not always much fun. It is of necessity about practice and repetition: about repeating a skill over and over again until it becomes subconscious. In those subject areas that require physical discipline, these movements become part of a person's physical memory, and can be effectively ignored during the creative process. Similarly, in those areas that rely more on mental discipline, these techniques must become ingrained into the intellect. Of course, many disciplines will require a combination of both physical and mental agility. The acquisition of physical techniques can actually be a highly meditative experience – the scales are practised without the need for thought, pliés are performed without requiring any intellectual input. The mind is left free to wander, or simply to lie still, while the body is at work.

Acquiring technique is about becoming comfortable and experienced with the medium in which you are expressing yourself. The actual medium that we use will be specific to the form of expression we are undertaking. In many instances, particularly in the performing arts, the medium of expression is that person's own body. Dancers, musicians and actors must all maintain their bodies to the necessary levels of condition (whether whole body, hands, voice). Some people's bodies are clearly suited to a particular form of expression – a dancer who cannot naturally do the splits will have trouble achieving some of the more extreme positions. However, lacking certain physical assets does not necessarily mean these people will be less creative – we can certainly fight against our natural limitations.

Of course, beyond any mastery of our physical selves that is required, we must also master other aspects of our discipline. For the ballerina this will involve hours of pointe work until her feet are sufficiently strengthened; for the sculptor this will mean mastering a variety of tools and materials; for the scientist it will be necessary to learn how to conduct experiments in a safe and fair way.

Although technique is important in shaping and structuring a piece of creative work, it is of equal importance to 'hide' the technique from the audience. In other words – it's meant to look easy, even though it isn't! This is particularly so in the performing arts – a dancer will be using huge quantities of physical effort, but her movements should appear relaxed and easy in front of the audience; an actor must commit large chunks of text to memory, yet appear to say them on stage for the very first time. The ability to hide the technique will help the audience to feel relaxed, allowing them to enjoy themselves as they interact with the creative piece. This is one of the key reasons why technique is actually important – we don't want anyone to spot any errors, because these will get in between the audience and what has been created.

In some instances, all the technical ability in the world will still leave the audience feeling cold – understanding and using technique is never the same as harnessing creativity. Although the creative person must understand, and be able to use, technique, it is only important because it allows the creativity to take place. There will even be occasions when the creative journey involves understanding traditional techniques, but only so that they can be thrown away. Some of the most inspired creative works of the last century were those where traditional techniques were effectively destroyed – the experimental dance pieces of Pina Bausch or the cubist paintings of Pablo Picasso. Once again, creativity can mean walking a path that is way ahead of what is currently viewed as 'acceptable', and this includes attitudes to the disciplines involved.

The 'chuck or keep?' question

Creativity is as much about what we decide to leave out as what we choose to put in. What I call 'chuck or keep?' questions will occur and reoccur at various points during the creative journey. These are the points at which, faced with limitless possibilities over what to include, the creative person must make a decision about whether to chuck something away or keep it. It could be deciding whether to keep a single idea or image. It might be finding ourselves heading down a blind alley in our thinking. It could even be looking at the results of the entire creative journey and saying 'that just doesn't work for me'.

When these 'chuck or keep?' questions occur, we can be hit by various feelings that will get in the way of the correct creative decision. We might think 'I don't want to waste this great idea', even though we can see that it doesn't fit into this particular piece. We could have the feeling that 'I've put loads of time and effort into this so it must be worth keeping.' There are clearly going to be different levels of perfectionism – different standards that each individual is willing to accept. However, a willingness to throw away what doesn't work is vital for the integrity of the creative person. For every finished picture that an artist sends out into the world, there might be fifty versions which did not make it; for every new idea that a scientist proposes, there could be fifty other concepts that were tried and tested, and found wanting.

When we have been working for a long time on a creative piece, we tend to get very close to it – so much so that we might feel an urge to throw it away, even though it actually works very well. It can be difficult to step back from the work and take an objective overview because we have been living with that piece at such close proximity. At this stage it can be very useful to put it away for a while, in a literal or metaphorical bottom drawer, and then return to it with fresh eyes at a later date. That way we get a better impression of how an outside observer will react on first viewing the piece.

In education the urge to have 'something' to assess can really snag against the creative journey. 'Is that finished?' we demand of our students, snatching a half-dried painting from their hands in our desperation to have some samples of their work to 'prove' what they've done. Perhaps we too might benefit from using a 'bottom drawer' in which our children can keep all the creative pieces that they produce over the course of a school year. They could then look back at these towards the end of the year and consider which they are proud to keep, which might need or deserve reworking, and which can be consigned to the bin.

The 'stop!' moment

When we undertake a creative endeavour, we are involved in striving for the very best that we can possibly achieve. We constantly search for what is perfect, true, or most delightful – hunting for the ultimate in creativity. However, that search could continue *ad infinitum*, and we might never actually get to where we're going. If we are going to be creative we must also accept that sometimes we will have to settle for less than total perfection – that we've got find the best fit or the best result that we possibly can, knowing when to say 'enough is enough'. In addition, there will be times when we get caught up in endlessly working and reworking a piece, so much so that it starts to go downhill rather than improving.

Any attempt at creativity will inevitably involve playing a percentages game, and every individual's opinion of what is 'finished' will vary widely. For the perfectionist, an output of three or four masterpieces during a lifetime might be enough. On the other hand, many artists find themselves described as 'prolific'. They have so much to say that they are happy to send their creations out into the world perhaps a little bit unfinished, so that they can get on with creating the next one.

Perfectionism can get in the way of creativity, because the search for perfection means that little or nothing ever gets finished. This seems to be particularly the case for those artists whose very earliest works are hailed as 'masterpieces'. Perhaps the pressure of trying to live up to that first flash of genius in fact stifles the creative process. A good few years ago I read what is one of my favourite books of all time – Donna Tartt's *The Secret History*. I waited with baited breath for her to produce another, and was still waiting ten years later. (Thankfully she did finally get around to it, publishing *The Little Friend* in 2002.)

Knowing when to stop can be hard, but there will also come a point at which any further alterations or additions will actually make the end result of the creative journey worse rather than better. Of course, things are a bit more prosaic in the classroom, where the 'stop!' moment might well be dictated by the bell ringing for the end of the lesson.

Reflection

Finally, the creative process draws to a close and you achieve a 'finished result', or you realize that one will not be achieved this time around. At this stage it is tempting to send your creation off into the world and never to consider it again. In fact, evaluating what you have achieved will play a vital role in improving it (a chance that non-fiction writers are lucky enough to get when producing a second edition of a book). It will also help you to further your own creativity for the next time around.

When reflecting on the creative process, you might be looking back at the steps you took during the process of creation. You might also be looking at the end product to establish how satisfied you and others are with it. It can be tempting to be overly critical of our finished creative endeavours: perhaps our fear of how others will react means that we get in first with our own criticisms.

With the children that we teach, we need to achieve a happy

medium. We want them to reflect on and evaluate what they have done, so that they can make improvements next time around. However, we also want them to feel a sense of pride in their achievements, and a willingness to move onto the next thing. In the classroom, we might encourage positive reflection by:

- Asking our students to keep a journal or diary during the creative journey and, when they have finished the piece, to look back at the steps they took. You might ask them to think about which parts of the journey were most successful, and where they could have made improvements.
- Sharing the work around the class, and asking each child to make one positive comment about it, if possible developing the comment to include specifics (e.g. 'I really like the way you've used bright colours in this painting, it gives me a really happy feeling').
- Putting the children in groups and asking them to:
  - Show their piece to the group.
  - Get one positive comment from each group member.
  - Talk about what they personally found hard/easy about the process.
  - Talk about what they found most interesting about working on the piece.
  - Talk about what they learned that could be applied next time around.
- Talking with the class about which pieces have been most successful in terms of technique, and which in terms of creativity.
- Displaying samples of the creative piece on your walls: either the ones that the class felt were most successful or simply the work of every child in the group.
- Keeping a series of finished pieces during the year, and subsequently looking back at these to reflect on the progression that the student has made in his or her creativity.

The process in a group

Working creatively in a group can be a very valuable experience for our students; it can also be very tricky to get it right. Genuinely collaborative work is perhaps the hardest of all creative journeys to undertake. Incorporating the different opinions and ideas of a range of people into one creative piece is bound to be hard. In the world outside of school, it will quite often be the case that one person takes on the role of directing a creative collaboration, making key decisions for the group. For instance, in a film the director will have responsibility for overall creative decisions.

When setting our children to work in a group there are various practical issues that we need to consider, and to find ways of overcoming. You might experience problems with:

- Ensuring that all members of the group contribute in a reasonably equal way.
- The temptation for the most confident group member to take over, and start acting as 'creative director'. (Note: This is not necessarily a 'bad' thing. However, in school we are obviously trying to give opportunities for all our children to take a reasonably equal part.)
- Squabbles that arise as the children fight for their own ideas to be used.
- Lots of noise (not necessarily negative!) as the students argue over the potential of different ideas.
- Too much noise, which means that the children find it difficult to concentrate, or even to hear each other.
- The quieter children opting out, because they have less confidence in putting the case for their own ideas.
- Genuinely creative ideas getting quashed because the children are fearful of taking risks.
- Having too much material in the 'improvisation stage', and finding it difficult to decide what to cut and what to keep.
- The tendency for the students to drift off task as time goes by.
- Agreeing on a 'finished' end product.

It is not necessarily straightforward for us as teachers to overcome these problems. However, it is worth remembering that group efforts at creativity will *always* be tricky – inside the school and outside as well. A good part of the learning involved in group creativity is to do with the skills of cooperation and consideration. Whether or not the work culminates in a wonderful 'end result' should perhaps be the least of our concerns.

A key part of the teacher's responsibility is to 'police' the creative efforts – to add structure and control to what can become a chaotic and even argumentative situation. Here are some thoughts about how you might do this.

- *Set clear objectives*: Although we don't want to iron all the chaos and freedom out of the creative process, we are obviously constrained by the time available in the lesson/school day. This means that we do need to ensure that our children work with sufficient focus, and setting a clear target will help keep them on track. Our objectives could be both for the end result of the creative process and also for each lesson during a period of creativity. For instance, you might set an objective in one lesson of 'coming up with at least ten different ideas to consider in the next session.'
- *Give a structure for contributions*: You will probably find that some of your students do tend to take over when put into group situations. If this is the case, then it is a good idea to give the children a specific structure for their contributions. To give an example, you might set a time limit of two minutes for each individual to offer his or her own ideas to the group in turn.
- *Use a 'conch'*: Using a 'conch' offers an excellent way of avoiding the situation where all the group members attempt to contribute their ideas or opinions simultaneously. The idea of a 'conch' is borrowed from the book *Lord of the Flies*, in which a group of children are trapped on a deserted island, and try to set up a democratic society. They use a conch shell during their group meetings – the person holding the shell is allowed to speak without interruption. This idea can usefully be adapted to use in the classroom. Give each group a conch (this can be any precious-looking object or item) and explain that when one child is holding it, the others must let that person have his or her say.
- *Work with individual talents*: Try to set up a situation where children with different individual talents can contribute in their own ways. If one child is a very able writer, he might be the designated note taker. If another child is particularly good at drawing, then she could make a visual representation of

their ideas. In this way, each child can offer his or her own skills or abilities to the mixture, and in so doing achieve a feeling of success. The teacher can facilitate this use of individual talents by setting creative activities that require a range of different skills – writing, drawing, practical work, and so on.

- *Incorporate sharing times*: It can be very useful to have times during the course of the lesson when the groups stop work to share their ideas with the class as a whole. The feedback might be a case of each group summarizing what has been done so far; it could be one group sharing a 'shaft of light' idea with the whole class.

- *Try the short, sharp approach*: Although achieving a finished creative project will typically take plenty of time, there will be some occasions when a great deal can be learned from some short, sharp creative efforts. When using group collaborations, this could mean giving the children only a very short time within each group, before swapping them around. This will give them a chance to practise in different group settings, and it will also help them retain their focus and stay on task. At the end of the lesson you might like to work with the class to examine which ideas or initial pieces are worth pursuing, and which are unlikely to lead anywhere and can be thrown away.

- *Spread out*: The constraints of classroom space can get in the way of some of our messier or more resource-intensive efforts at creativity. If the age and maturity of your students allows, and if there are other free spaces available, then you might consider allowing at least some of your groups to go off and work in another place. If you have one or more assistants working with you in your lessons, then these other members of staff could help supervise the various groups. Taking this approach requires a high level of trust from the teacher – both that the students will behave themselves, and also that they won't just go off task the minute they leave the room. If your students are genuinely motivated by and interested in the work they are doing, then having a space of their own in which to work can help maximize their levels of concentration and commitment. (Note: It is important to remember that, as teacher, you are responsible for the students at all times while they are under your supervision. Please do not try this if you have any concerns over safety.) Another way of spreading out might be to take your class into a big space to work – the hall, or even outdoors if the weather allows.

When collaborating, your students might be working together to develop a single piece in one particular medium, or they might be collaborating across different media or even through different subject areas. Why not try developing some cross-curricular themes within your school, and collaborating with other teachers and classes on some creative pieces? Depending on the theme involved, there are many different possibilities. Subjects that typically work well together include dance, music and art, or science, design and technology and craft. However, there is clearly potential for plenty of creativity in the kind of collaborations you try out.

As well as collaborating within lesson time, there are also plenty of great opportunities to work in various group sizes on a wider, whole-school basis. Any form of public presentation, whether a school production, an arts event, or a sports demonstration, offers many chances for creativity in all sorts of different subjects. For more thoughts on these whole-school creative journeys, see Chapter 7.

3 The creative child

It is all that the young can do for the old, to shock them and keep them up to date.

George Bernard Shaw

At the heart of any creative endeavour lies the creative person. As teachers, we are especially privileged to work creatively with young people – we get the chance to perceive the world through the eyes of our children. At the very earliest age, our youngsters will hopefully still look at life with a sense of wonder and awe. Watching children make those first discoveries of how things work, and of how they can express themselves, would warm the heart of even the most hardened cynic. Sadly, though, it seems to be more and more the case that adult cynicism sets in very quickly.

Working with young people has a great way of keeping us young at heart. As we grow older, it is very tempting to deride the 'youth of today', and to hark back to what things were like in the 'good old days'. As teachers, we need to remember that what appears new and even shocking to us is in fact often the next generation simply finding creative and innovative ways of expressing themselves.

In this chapter I explore how early creativity might be encouraged or destroyed, talking in detail about what is meant by a 'creative frame of mind'. I also examine what I call the 'creative senses' – a range of ways in which children might perceive their world and which will feed into their creative expression. I talk about the role of imagination in some detail, looking at what it is and how the teacher might develop the imagination of his or her students. Finally, I look at how creativity can help those children with special needs, and those students whose behaviour is euphemistically termed 'challenging'.

Early creativity

Of course, as teachers, our hope is that our students will have been encouraged to be creative in the home environment, long before they arrive at school. The earliest years of a child's life provide a very fertile ground for the development of creative attitudes and approaches. The attitudes and abilities which are learned and developed in those first few years will often play a crucial part in later success. The creativity of very young children might be developed in a whole variety of ways.

- Being surrounded by books, pictures, music, etc. and seeing their parents or guardians interact with these on a regular basis.
- Learning from the parental role model in behaving and thinking creatively within the home and beyond.
- Being encouraged to explore their own creativity from an early age, for instance through imaginative play.
- Having a range of resources in the home that encourage the expression of creativity – paints, play dough, toys that involve using the imagination.
- Being given access to potentially creative experiences – going to singing classes, taking dance lessons, visiting art galleries, trips away, and so on.
- Learning and practising the techniques of creativity – imaginative thinking, playing the piano, reading stories, etc.
- Responding to the child's efforts at creativity with enthusiasm and praise rather than discouragement and negativity.

In the home environment there are many factors that can mitigate against the development of creativity. For a start, it can be very messy and time consuming to take part in creative activities with our children. In addition, the lure of the television and computer games is ever present. Many parents have so many demands on their time that developing creativity might come towards the bottom of the list. School can and should offer every child an environment in which there is the time, space and opportunity for the creative expression that might be lacking at home.

Unfortunately, at times during our teaching careers we will also come across children whose innate sense of creativity has been more seriously dampened or damaged. Perhaps they have not been given sufficient stimulus during their early years of life; perhaps their efforts at creativity have been criticized and derided. For these children, a key part of our work as teachers will be in repairing their confidence and self-esteem.

A creative frame of mind

As I pointed out in the first chapter, my belief is that creativity is as much about a frame of mind and an attitude to life's challenges as it is about a specific activity or product. The two are inextricably tied together: the process is as much about the attitude of the person or persons involved as about what they actually do or the creative outcomes which result. What, then, do I mean by a creative frame of mind, and how will this manifest itself in the children we teach? The approaches or attitudes that will need to be nurtured to develop a child's creativity will include some or all of the following:

- *Curious*:
  - Why does it work like that?
  - Does it really work how everyone says it does?
  - What if I tried doing this instead?
  - How about if I put this and this together?
- *Questioning*:
  - What's this all about?
  - What would happen if . . .?
  - How can I overcome this problem?
  - How can I look at this differently?
  - Is this necessarily 'right' just because it's normally accepted?
  - What difficulties might this throw up?
- *Imaginative*:
  - How does this look in my mind's eye?
  - What are the different possibilities here?
  - What alternatives can I try out?
- *Sensory*:
  - How can I use my senses to respond to this?
  - Which of my senses does this most engage?

- What can I see/hear/taste/touch/smell here?
- How do I feel about my sensory reactions to this?

- *Adventurous*:
  - What can I try that is new and unusual?
  - Can I take this one step beyond what has ever been before?
  - Shall I try doing this, or this, or this?
- *Rebellious*:
  - Do I really care what people think about this?
  - How can I shock people – make them sit up and think?
  - Am I willing to go against what everyone else does/says/ thinks?
- *Original*:
  - How can I approach this in a new or novel way?
  - What's a more unusual way of doing this?
  - Can I do this in a surprising way?
  - What's my own personal take on this?
- *Flexible*:
  - Is there more than one answer to this question?
  - Could it be that more than one of these answers is 'right'?
  - Does this have to make sense in a rational way?
  - What if I try looking at this in a completely different way?
- *Intuitive*:
  - What's my gut reaction to this?
  - What do I feel about this?
  - What do my instincts say?
  - Does it feel right?
  - Does it feel wrong?
- *Perceptive*:
  - How does this make me feel?
  - Am I letting my emotions override my logic?
  - How would this make other people feel?
  - Can I see something here that no one else has seen?
  - Where might this lead me?
  - Do I really want to go there?
- *Playful*:
  - What would happen if I tried this?
  - How about if I put this and this together?
  - What might happen if I do this?
  - Can I try doing this in a new way?

- *Able to find connections*:
  - How can I link these things together?
  - How do these ideas relate to each other?
  - Does this connect with anything done before?
  - Is there a pattern or trend to this?
  - Can I find any unusual connections here?
- *Decisive*:
  - What's the best way to do this?
  - Can I do this in another, better, way?
  - Do I feel that this is 'good enough'?
  - Is it time to ditch the lot and start again?
  - Which bits of this are most interesting?
  - What should I cut?
  - What should I keep?
- *Open minded*:
  - Is this necessarily right or best?
  - Can I see this as a challenge rather than as a problem?
  - What 'could be' potentially?
  - Do I need to throw this away?
  - What other options are there?
  - What other approaches might I try?
  - How will other people view this?
  - How can I see this from a variety of different viewpoints?
- *Risk taking*:
  - Am I brave enough to try this?
  - I wonder what would happen if I do this?
  - Can I put aside fears about what other people might say/ think/believe?
- *Reflective*:
  - How well does this work?
  - Can I make it work better?
  - How can I adapt or modify this?
  - What other points of view might there be on this?
  - What works well in someone else's piece of work?
  - How might I learn from what he/she has done?

The creative senses

One of the key facets of creativity is an ability to apply our senses to the world around us. We then bring our sensory responses into the creative piece we are shaping, translating our own perception of the world into the medium within which we are working. These perceptions of the world are very much our own – it is not possible to get someone else to step into our minds or bodies and see or understand the world in exactly the same way that we do. So it is that our creative endeavours become a way of expressing ourselves – showing other people how we personally perceive the world around us.

I'd like to propose that we, and of course the children we teach, have a number of what I call 'creative senses'. Any creative journey will involve using some or even all of these senses. They are related to the five main senses with which we are all so familiar: sight, sound, touch, taste and smell. They arise out of our use of the five senses, but many of them fall under more than one of these headings. (For instance, you might hear the tone of a piece of music, but you could also see tone within a picture or piece of writing.)

These creative senses are also related to the 'multiple intelligences' identified by Howard Gardner. Gardner's work has led to the proposal that different children learn best in different ways or 'styles'. We can certainly see this at work in the classroom, for instance some children prefer visual approaches, while others like to learn through active, practical work. Similarly, if we were to say the word 'dog' to a class of students, some children would respond by talking about what a dog looks like, others by focusing on the sounds a dog would make, others on the texture of its fur. These learning styles can also feed into our lessons, so that we might include visual, auditory and kinaesthetic activities to appeal to different children's preferred ways of working.

When we are involved in creativity, we will be applying a range of our creative senses to the activity at hand. Some creative activities will lend themselves more towards using certain of these senses. For instance, a chef putting together a new recipe will make particular use of his sense of taste, texture and scent to find the best possible taste for the meal. He might also utilize his sense of colour, shape and proportion to ensure that the finished meal looks, as well as tastes, beautiful. Even within the same subject, different children will use different combinations of these creative senses. One child might approach a piece of art with a strong sense of colour and shape; another could approach the same artwork with more of a sense of pattern and space.

The 'creative senses' that we might endeavour to develop and explore will include, in no particular order, a sense of:

- Pattern
- Shape
- Colour
- Shade
- Melody
- Pitch
- Tone
- Order
- Volume
- Proportion
- Texture
- Taste
- Scent
- Space
- Rhythm
- Motion
- Direction
- Flow
- Pace
- Size
- Mood
- Emotion
- Weight
- Duality
- Style
- Something beyond (sometimes called the 'sixth sense').

In the classroom, our children will be applying a wide range of these creative senses to the creative work that they do right across the curriculum. The more of these senses we can encourage them to apply, the better the results will be. Let's look at an example of a creative piece, to see how some of these senses might be applied.

Writing a story
- *Pattern*: repetition of certain key words.
- *Shape*: the overall 'shape' of the storyline, the peaks and troughs of tension within the piece.
- *Shade*: using words to give a sense of light and dark within the story.
- *Tone*: creating a tone of voice, for instance excitement, by the choice of vocabulary and sentence structure.
- *Order*: deciding on the appropriate order in which plot events should come, exploring to see which word order works best.
- *Rhythm*: creating a sense of rhythm in the way that the words are ordered, through the choice of language and punctuation, and perhaps through the use of some internal rhymes.
- *Motion*: giving a sense of the story moving forwards to a conclusion.
- *Pace*: using sentence length and structure, punctuation, and an action-packed story, to keep the reader engrossed.
- *Mood*: creating a particular mood through choice of vocabulary and a sense of setting.
- *Emotion*: letting the characters' emotions come through by the way that they act and speak; allowing the author's emotional responses to the subject to emerge in the way that he or she writes.
- *Style*: incorporating a sense of personal style through the writer's voice, perhaps subverting traditional expectations of a genre.

The world of the imagination

There is nothing more difficult for a truly creative painter than to paint a rose, because before he can do so he has first to forget all the roses that were ever painted.

Henri Matisse

What is imagination?
Imagination is essentially creating something in your mind that isn't really there. It is the 'willing suspension of disbelief' – a pretence of or belief in something that doesn't really exist. When they are tiny, babies explore the world through their senses (as any parent

will know, mainly through putting things in their mouths). Before they are a year old, though, they begin to exhibit signs of imagination. A toddler will happily play 'rodeo' on your back, bouncing up and down on the parental 'horse'. He does not really *believe* that daddy has turned into a horse, but he is more than willing to take part in the pretence.

Children's early imaginative facilities can be very powerful: the fear of an imaginary monster under the bed can be so strong that a child refuses to switch off the light. As we grow older, we realize that these imaginary monsters do not really exist, although many people will retain the ability to believe in things that they cannot see (for instance, a god). Our ability to see things in our mind's eye allows us to enjoy stories of all kinds – whether in novels, at the theatre or on television. The power of imagination is increasingly being harnessed to enhance performance, for instance the sports person who visualizes himself scoring a goal or winning a race.

Why is imagination important?
Of course, like all creative endeavours, imaginative activity can be a lot of fun. But it is of course much more than this, and it plays a crucial part in our ability to think creatively. Imagination is important because:

- It gives us access to creativity – allowing us to imagine in our mind's eye, and then bring into being, things that have not existed before.
- It can help us to harness our fear of the unknown, and to decide what we personally do and do not believe.
- It allows us to make the mental leap in which we see that one thing can stand for, or pretend to 'be', something else. This gives us the foundation from which we are later able to understand the symbolic languages of humankind – numbers, symbolism, linguistic imagery, and so on.
- It allows us to picture worlds above or beyond our own – ones that do not necessarily exist. The castles of fairy stories, alien planets, heaven and hell.
- It enables us to imagine experiences that we might not yet have had, or that we may never have – flying like a bird over fields and forests, sailing a ship across a mountainous sea.

- It helps us to propose and formulate new ideas and inventions – the aeroplane, the spaceship, the computer.
- It allows us to translate one form of sensory perception into another – words in a book into pictures in our heads, music into images or movements, colours into emotions.
- It helps us understand better what it's like to be someone else, allowing us to empathize with other people's emotions, situations or viewpoints.
- It plays a key part in our own cultural understanding of the world: the myths and stories that have built our society and those of other cultures.
- It allows us to find new questions for which answers could be found, beyond that which we already know or understand.

What gets in the way of imagination?
Unfortunately, there are plenty of things that can get in the way of us using our imaginations. Although young children are normally very willing to use their imaginative powers, the teacher will still encounter plenty of barriers that need to be overcome. This is particularly so as the little darlings we teach get a bit older and become more susceptible to external pressures. Here's a quick rundown of some of the things that might get in the way of a child's imaginative powers.

- A fear about what others might think.
- The feeling that we are being a bit stupid or daft.
- The perception that this kind of pretence is childish.
- The power that peer pressure plays in creating these concerns.
- The way that schools and schooling are organized (i.e. the focus on structure and rational thought).
- Getting pulled into emulating the imaginative journeys of other people.
- Toys that leave little room for the imagination.

Developing the imagination
What is now proved was once only imagined.

William Blake

There are plenty of ways in which we can help our children develop their imaginations. These approaches can be incorporated into any lesson as a warm-up or starter activity, or could be used to develop more extended pieces of work. Here are some suggestions to get you started.

- *The circle of imagination*: Ask the class to stand in a circle and pass around some invisible objects. The children should interact with these to help them appear 'real'. You might pass around an animal, a heavy box, a fragile book, a ticking bomb.
- *Throwing the imaginary ball*: Get your students throwing a ball across the circle, making eye contact with the person to whom they are throwing before it leaves their hands.
- *Discarded clothes*: Put a set of clothes or a costume on your classroom floor. Talk with the children about who discarded these clothes, why they have been left behind, and where that person has gone. Work together to build an imaginary character, perhaps acting out his or her last few minutes in the room.
- *The upside down room*: Get your children to move across the floor as though the room has tipped upside down (i.e. they are crawling across the ceiling).
- *The goalie*: Ask the students to stand in a space and act as a goalie in a football match. Their actions should follow the progress of the game (wincing as the other team scores a goal, preparing to catch the ball as it comes down their end).
- *Unreal insults*: Working in pairs, get the students to insult each other but using nonsense words, e.g. 'you're a purple headed fliggerbuzz' – 'yeah, but you're a stumblewonded biddlydod!'

Creativity and special needs

You can learn many things from children. How much patience you have, for instance.

Franklin P. Jones

For those children who have special educational needs, school might seem like one long struggle to access the curriculum. This is perhaps particularly so for those students who struggle with literacy – so much of the school day involves reading or writing in one form or another. For these children, creative activities can offer a chance for success and self-expression that does not exist elsewhere within the school. Being creative will also offer them some moments of relative relaxation.

I'm sure that you too will have noticed how some children who switch off or misbehave in the academic subjects suddenly prove themselves motivated and able at a school sports day or in a school production. As a teacher of both English and drama, I have seen startling differences in the same child when teaching each of my subjects. In English, those with poor literacy struggle to express themselves and communicate what they mean; in drama, their eyes light up as the class responds positively to a performance.

The arts subjects can be very beneficial for children with special needs. In drama, they might be playing a character who is confident and successful, and this can feed into their own lives outside the drama class. In art, a child might discover a real talent for the use of paint, which helps to build her self-confidence. In the music room or school recording studio, a student might find that he has a talent for rapping.

Creativity and behaviour

Violence among young people is an aspect of their desire to create. They don't know how to use their energy creatively so they do the opposite and destroy.

Anthony Burgess

As a so-called 'expert' on managing behaviour, when I found the quote above from Anthony Burgess it really made me sit up and think. So much of the misbehaviour we see is indeed very destructive. Sometimes it's about destroying the learning, either in a metaphorical way (refusing to listen, refusing to work) or in a literal way (throwing chairs, tearing down displays). Teachers also come across self-destructive behaviour – children who contain so much anger that they end up turning it in on themselves.

If we consider for a moment some of the reasons behind the challenging behaviour that we face as teachers, then we might begin to see how creativity can help us in improving behaviour. Harnessing creativity can aid us in managing difficult behaviour in a better way, and it can also help us make life better for those children whose anger manifests itself in destructive impulses. Below are just a few of the reasons why you might experience difficult behaviour, and some thoughts about how creativity can help you make the situation better.

- *Boredom*: Creative teaching techniques can help engage the students with the work, for instance making use of props or building simulations (see pp. 93–102).
- *Disaffection*: Creativity can help us find ways of making school seem relevant to those who don't see the point. Again, simulations offer a great way of doing this because they simulate the real lives of our students outside of school.
- *Low self-esteem*: Being shown that they can express themselves in a positive, creative manner and achieve really good results can boost the self-esteem of those with little confidence.
- *Inability to access the curriculum*: Teachers can use creative approaches to offer the class different ways of accessing the curriculum, for instance the concrete ways of explaining concepts described on p. 70.

4 The creative teacher

You need chaos in your soul to give birth to a dancing star.

Friedrich Nietzsche

As an environment, school is not particularly conducive to the chaos described in this quote from Nietzsche. You have probably noticed very few dancing stars in your career as a teacher. Our educational system seems to be far more concerned with structure and restraint than with freedom and anarchy. The constant stream of initiatives from above can leave us with little time or incentive to harness our own creative powers in the classroom. However, it is my belief that taking a creative approach to the job is absolutely vital: both for our own sakes and for those of our children.

In this chapter I give advice and practical strategies that will help you become a more creative teacher. I look at what a 'creative teacher' actually is, and I explore some of the reasons why it is important to incorporate creativity into your teaching. I look at practical ways in which you can incorporate creativity into those mundane, everyday classroom tasks, such as taking the register. I also look at the teacher as a role model of creativity for his or her students, and at how you might share examples of your own creative endeavours with your class. Finally, I look again at the subject of 'finding a balance' – ways in which we can sensibly balance Nietzsche's search for 'chaos' with the daily realities of the classroom.

What is a creative teacher?

What we want is to see the child in pursuit of knowledge, and not knowledge in pursuit of the child.

George Bernard Shaw

The NACCCE report on creativity (*All Our Futures: Creativity, Culture and Education* — see p. 135 for further details) identifies two strands relating to creativity and the teacher's classroom practice. These are 'teaching creatively' and 'teaching for creativity'. In other words, there is a difference between us approaching the job in a creative manner and actually finding ways to develop our students' creativity.

My belief is that when a person teaches with a creative frame of mind, this is almost honour bound to filter through into what happens in his or her classroom. It strikes me that it would be nigh on impossible to espouse and use creative approaches ourselves, while failing to incorporate them into the way in which we help our children to learn. A genuinely creative approach to life will filter through into every aspect of our lives: the way that we talk, move, explain, interact, and so on and on.

Above all else, the creative teacher will light a fire within his or her children: making the whole process of learning seem worth while and exciting. As Shaw recommends, rather than chasing after our students with a whole bundle of facts, skills and techniques, what we need to do instead is inspire the children to want to find out about and achieve these things for themselves. While I am not espousing a situation where children only learn through discovery, we certainly need to find a better balance between that and the instructive 'by rote' mode that dominates at the present time.

The creative teacher will of course take a creative frame of mind in relation to his or her work. The various attitudes and approaches that I identified in the third chapter of this book ('The creative child', see pp. 46–8) will all come into play. He or she will take a creative frame of mind in planning and teaching lessons, and will also encourage the children to utilize that same frame of mind in their own work. Using the same list of creative attributes given in Chapter 3, here are some thoughts about how you might apply these approaches to help you become a more creative teacher.

- *Curious*: Retaining that essential curiosity about how and why things work in the way that they do. Maintaining this childlike attitude towards the job reminds us what teaching is actually all about (that is, inspiring a love of learning). It also helps us to ward off the cynicism that can so easily creep in with the pressures of our work. Our own innate sense of interest and curiosity will feed into the way that we teach our children – not only in what we say and do but in *how* we say and do it.

- *Questioning*: Constantly questioning the way that things are, or the way that things are accepted to be. Looking for interesting questions within a particular subject or topic area, and posing these as puzzles for the children to examine. Using open-ended rather than closed questions in our lessons: 'Why do you think it works like this?' rather than 'Which of these is the right answer?' Refusing to simply 'accept' that we should teach certain things in a certain way – constantly questioning the status quo.

- *Imaginative*: Finding unusual or imaginative ways to introduce topics, and also imaginative ways to engage the children. Harnessing the power of our own and our children's imagination in relation to both factual and fictional topics.

- *Sensory*: Finding ways of delivering our lessons that encourage the children to use all their different senses. Considering our own typical sensory responses to a stimulus, and trying to widen these out beyond the 'norm'. Creating a classroom environment that appeals to all the senses, including the 'creative senses' identified in the last chapter.

- *Adventurous*: Going a step beyond what might typically be expected. Experimenting with new approaches and ideas. Being a bit 'ahead of our time' because we respond to our own intuition rather than simply accepting tradition.

- *Rebellious*: Fighting the urge to always 'follow the pack' – refusing to let 'we've always done it that way' be a good enough reason for us to follow suit. Kicking back against authority or authoritarian approaches and being a bit subversive (or even a lot!).

- *Original*: Offering a unique and innovative style of teaching. Teaching in a way that the children might describe as 'a bit off the wall', a bit different. Having the courage to try out unusual approaches or ideas, to see where they might lead, without constantly worrying about what might go wrong, or about what other people will think.

- *Flexible*: Spotting a good lead when the children offer it to us. Letting the children dictate the direction of their own learning as and when appropriate. Having the flexibility to adapt a lesson while it is actually taking place, so that it better suits the children's learning.

- *Intuitive*: Going with our gut instincts at times – listening to our intuitions as well as to our more rational selves. Trusting our intuition about how to respond to individual students – who needs the gentle hand of encouragement, and who will respond well to a tougher line.
- *Perceptive*: Seeing school and learning from the children's perspective. Having a sense of how they will react to a lesson before it is delivered. Being perceptive about the children's potential responses to a particular topic or activity – understanding which methods and approaches will suit them best.
- *Playful*: Remembering, and being willing, to be a 'big kid' at times. Having some fun and letting the children have fun as well. Playing around with ideas, resources, a variety of approaches, and so on.
- *Able to find connections*: Constantly looking for connections – both in a way that will help the children learn, and so that these links can be pointed out to the class. Looking for connections between the children's behaviour and the root causes of any problems. Analysing what we do in the classroom, how effectively it works and why.
- *Decisive*: Making on the spot decisions about the direction of a lesson. Knowing when to say 'enough' if an approach does not seem to be working as intended. Seeing problems as a positive challenge rather than a negative difficulty, and taking decisive action to overcome them.
- *Open minded*: Keeping our minds open to the new, the untried or the unusual. Seeing every situation from a number of different perspectives. Understanding the 'youth of today' and accepting the ways in which their perception and experiences of the world might differ from our own.
- *Risk taking*: Having the courage to take risks in our planning, or in our classroom practice. Accepting that when we try out something new, things won't always go according to plan. Retaining the humility to keep learning from our mistakes.
- *Reflective*: Looking back at what has happened in the past, to try and find ways of improving things in the future. Analysing

both the end product and the process involved in the teacher's work. Being willing to reflect on success and failure, and to learn from each equally.

Why be a creative teacher?

There are many benefits in becoming a more creative teacher. Applying a sense of creativity to our work will benefit us personally. It will furthermore allow us to improve our classroom practice, and it will also be of great advantage to the children that we teach. In brief, being a creative teacher will help us:

- Maintain drive and motivation in the work that we do.
- Find ways of constantly improving and developing our teaching.
- Fight against the stress and cynicism that can creep into our attitude to our work, especially for those who teach particularly challenging children.
- Make our work more interesting, exciting and personally fulfilling.
- Make our working lives easier, for instance harnessing creativity to find unusual methods of managing the classroom.
- Ensure the classroom is an interesting place for our children to be.
- Engage the children more fully in their learning.
- Be involved in developing the creative potential of the next generation.
- Have lots of fun!

Everyday creativity

There are a large number of relatively mundane tasks that must be done in the classroom – tasks that you might think offer little opportunity for developing creativity. However, with a bit of lateral thought these activities can help the teacher incorporate lots of opportunities for creativity. These will inevitably make your classroom a more interesting place in which to be. And by taking a creative approach we also effectively demonstrate to our children how a creative frame of mind can be adopted in pretty much any set of circumstances. Hopefully, the infectiousness of your own efforts at creativity will transmit itself to your students. As well as thinking up ideas of your own, don't forget to let your children contribute as well. Here are some suggestions to get you started.

- *Setting up your room*: Teachers will often set up their classrooms right at the start of the first term, and then leave the room layout pretty much untouched for the rest of the year. This is a shame – to encourage your children to think imaginatively and laterally, it is well worth keeping them on their toes. If they arrive at your room and find that the layout has changed, this will help them view your lessons with a fresh sense of perspective. You could try:
  - Completely changing the layout of seating at the start of the year. This is especially effective if you have inherited a classroom from another teacher. Making changes before the children first arrive will help establish the space as your own.
  - Consider whether rows or groups of tables will be most effective in encouraging creativity (the latter will usually work best).
  - Do some furniture rearranging during your lessons. Although this takes a bit of time and organization, and at first it can be a bit noisy and chaotic, eventually your children will be 'trained' to do quick changes as and when required. You might move the tables to the sides of the room and create a U shape of seats for a debate. You could push all the furniture out of the way and get them sitting on the floor. Of course, if you share the room, be sure to return the furniture to its normal position at the end.
  - Head out into an alternative space for a whole lesson, or just for part of it. A change from indoors to outside can refresh a class whose concentration is dwindling; a move into the school hall will give you enough space to try out some movement activities.
- *Taking the register*: This is a job that can eat up a fair bit of time during the school day. Find ways to make it a bit more interesting and imaginative, for instance:

- Adapting the way you use your voice – taking the register loudly, quietly, with an accent, as a character, very quickly/ slowly, etc.
- Asking the children to answer with something other than their names, for instance the emotion that they are feeling at that moment, a number from one to ten to indicate how happy they are, and so on.
- Getting a child to take the register for you, perhaps offering this as a reward, or circulating the job so that everyone has a go.
- Doing the register backwards, so that those children whose surnames always place them at the end of the register have a chance to go first for a change.

• *Getting the class silent*: There will be any number of times during the average lesson that you will need to get your class silent, so that you can talk to them. I will often agree a specific silence signal with a class to save time and effort, and I know that many other teachers do the same. The silence signals that you utilize might work reasonably well if they are fairly mundane (although in a 'tough' school they might soon cease to be effective). However, children will typically respond much better to an unusual signal, or to a teacher who changes his or her silence signal regularly. Being a bit creative with your silence signals will help you motivate the class to keep watching out for your cues. Again, here are some suggestions for doing this:

- At the most basic level, raising a hand in the air or clapping three times, as a cue for the children to stop talking. However, there is plenty of scope for making things much more interesting.
- I sometimes do a 'staying alive' dance as a cue – seeing me do an impression of John Travolta always gets a laugh from the children. Admittedly you have to be brave/mad to try it.
- Standing on a chair or desk to gain the class's attention.
- Using a short blast of really powerful (and loud) music to stop the class in its tracks.
- I once heard about an art teacher who, when she wanted the class to be silent and listen, turned on a set of fairy lights

which she had taped around her whiteboard. What a wonderful idea!

- Another great idea, nicked from the *TES* staffroom forums, is to have some glittery 'quiet dust' available to sprinkle on your class.

- *Moving between activities*: There will be many times during the typical school day (particularly at primary level) when we need to move groups of children, or a whole class, between activities. Set up a more creative and imaginative impulse for moving and you will generally get a far better result. Here are some ideas for you to try:
  - Telling the children to move as though they are walking over a sleeping giant's back (i.e. as quietly as possible, so as not to wake him).
  - Asking the class to move as though they are part of a slow motion sequence in a film.
  - Telling the children to imagine they are floating across the room in zero gravity, preferably without bumping into each other.

- *Getting resources*: Again, there will be any number of times at which you will need some or all of the children to collect resources for their work. This can be a recipe for chaos and disaster if it is not well managed, so why not use a creative inspiration to encourage them to do it efficiently? You might try using the film *Kindergarten Cop* as an inspiration, and 'training' your children as though they are police recruits. On a signal from you, various 'teams' could be challenged to go and get their resources in the style of police cadets (i.e. very efficiently).

- *Ending the lesson*: The end of the lesson can potentially be a time when all hell breaks loose, as the bell goes and the students steam out of the room, leaving you standing amid chaos. (This is perhaps particularly so in some of the more messy, freeform, creative lessons. I still have a distinct memory of a nightmare drama lesson in which I had set an activity to make collages of different characters. When the bell went for break, I was left standing in the middle of my drama studio, with the floor completely covered in tiny scraps of cut out paper.) The tone set at the end of a lesson will often set the mood for the next time you see the class. In the secondary school, if you let a class head out in a 'mad mood', the teacher who they see next will not thank you. To finish your lessons in a calm and creative way, you might like to have a go at the 'statues' idea given below:

- I often use this 'statues' exercise to end my lessons. I frame it as a 'game' or a 'challenge' to the students, to make it seem more like fun than like work. The teacher says '3, 2, 1, freeze' and the children must then freeze completely still, like statues, for a set period of time (around 2 to 3 minutes is about right). During this time they may breathe (they will probably ask), but they should keep everything else still. Interestingly, if you try this exercise, you will probably notice a correlation between those children who exhibit really poor concentration in lessons and those who find it almost impossible to remain still. During the time that the children are frozen, you can give praise about the work, reminders about homework, or just take a welcome break. When the time is up, I finish the exercise by asking the children to put their chairs under their desks in slow motion.

The teacher as role model

Although at times it might not feel like it, the class teacher does generally provide a role model for the majority of his or her students. Even in a class full of disaffected youths, there will be many students who yearn for at least some sense of personal creativity. I am lucky enough to have the chance to talk with large numbers of different teachers. When I ask whether they too came into teaching (either generally, or of a specific subject) because of an inspirational teacher in their past, many of these teachers know exactly what I mean.

Having the chance to inspire your children is, surely, one of the finest things about our profession. To enable your children to recognize and develop their own creativity, and perhaps to inspire in them a lifelong passion for a subject, is a wonderful and important position to hold. As teachers, we can provide a role model for creativity by showing and hopefully sharing with our students:

- A passion for the whole learning experience.
- An excitement about the subject or subjects being taught.
- A delight in and for the creative process.
- A sense of wonder and excitement at the end products created during this process.

Teachers put across this passion, excitement, delight and wonder in many different ways. Above all, it will occur in the way that you communicate to the class, and also in the way that you react to each individual child's own creative efforts. To inspire our students, we need to use our faces, voices, energy and mood in a positive and enthusiastic way. Children will almost always respond to a sense of passion in their teachers, although on occasions the response might be 'are you feeling all right, miss/sir?'.

Sharing your creativity

One excellent way in which teachers can model creativity for their students is to show and use examples of their own creative work. This is an effective technique, both for the teacher him or herself and also for the children in our classes. It has many advantages, some of which I have listed below.

- *Fun and fulfilment*: Spending time on our own creativity gives us a chance to have some fun, and also to achieve a sense of personal fulfilment. A good part of the job of the teacher, particularly beyond the classroom, will be fairly routine and mundane (all that paperwork, for instance). Reminding ourselves of our own capabilities can help us recapture some of the joy of the job and give a welcome boost to our own self-esteem.
- *We can all be creative*: It demonstrates to the children that teachers can be creative too (we are human after all). The children will see that anyone, no matter what their job, can enjoy the creative process as part of their everyday lives. This will help your students get away from the image of the tortured artist, locked away in a garret.
- *A piece of myself*: The class gain a sense that the teacher is willing to open his or her own self to them – to show them a piece of the person behind or beyond the teacher. Putting

yourself 'on the line' in this way is a powerful demonstration of your commitment to the class. In a way, you are opening yourself up to the response of an audience – often a scary experience for the person involved.

- *Standing in their shoes*: Generally speaking, we spend much of our time assessing and perhaps criticizing what our students produce. It will always serve as a good leveller and an important learning experience to put ourselves in their shoes for a while.
- *Understanding the creative process*: Being involved in creating a piece for ourselves will help us better understand the processes and efforts that our students have to go through to produce a creative piece. It also demonstrates to us the kind of timescales that are required for all the stages of development during the building of a creative work.
- *Intellectualizing the creative process*: By producing a creative piece of our own, we can begin to intellectualize the stages and steps that are involved in creativity. The teacher can then work backwards from this point to show the children what they need to do to produce their own creative work.
- *Understanding audience responses*: Your sample can be used to demonstrate the ways in which audience responses may differ, and how judgement of value is a relative concept. Some of your students may view your creative effort as a masterpiece, while others may be a bit less certain about its worth.
- *Understanding the evaluative parts of creativity*: As an extension, and if you are brave, you might ask your students to evaluate what you have done. Again, this can be a very valuable learning experience as they pick apart the finished product to see how it was created and how effective the outcome has been.

The pieces of work you share with the class might be produced outside of the school environment, and can actually offer a rather relaxing break from marking, paperwork and the like. However, we can equally well join in during an activity that we set the class. For example, when you ask your children to brainstorm words to go into a poem, you might on occasions spend the time doing a brainstorm of your own. Seeing their teacher working alongside them in this way can be a powerful motivator and inspiration for the class.

In addition to showing your own 'finished products', it can also work well to show your children the various parts of your creative journey. This might mean showing them the mind-map that you created before writing a story or essay, or sharing the preparatory studies that you made prior to creating a finished work of art. The work that you share does not necessarily have to have been created recently. In the past I have also brought in some samples of my own schoolwork to share.

If you do not have sufficient time or motivation to produce your own creative work to share with the class, then it can also be effective to show a creative piece from a student you have taught in the past, although always ask the student's permission if possible. The piece doesn't even have to be particularly brilliant – we often learn as much from seeing what *doesn't* work as what does.

Intellectualizing creativity

To teach is to learn twice.

Joseph Joubert

One of the key skills of the teacher is the ability to walk *backwards* down the path to understanding. When a teacher sets out to teach a class about 'x' or 'y', he or she has probably/hopefully already arrived at the relevant destination. We know or understand how to do that thing for ourselves, but we need to pass on that knowledge or understanding to our children. So it is that, as teachers, we effectively need to learn all over again.

When we find a subject or skill relatively easy to do, it can be hard to see why or where the students might experience difficulties. In the primary classroom, we will often be teaching at a point that is many years below our actual level of understanding. For instance, when teaching addition to a class, we already know how to add up. Actually walking backwards to see how we originally learned this, and how we might make it readily understandable to the children, can be difficult. At secondary level, our specialism in a particular subject might mean that the various techniques and skills come naturally to us. In both age ranges, once we have been teaching for a number of years, we may have taught a topic so many times that understanding it seems blindingly obvious to us.

The key is to intellectualize the processes involved in the journey, so that we can break down the steps and stages we have used and pass these on to our students. As a teacher, there have been many occasions when I've been struggling to help my students understand how to undertake a specific activity, for instance, writing an essay. At these times, I have found it incredibly useful to do the activity myself before the lesson and, as I do so, to consider the intellectual steps and processes that I am taking. In this way I can hopefully find simple, effective and creative ways of passing on my knowledge to the class. If our intention is to develop greater creativity in our students, then we are going to have to enhance our own creativity in the process.

Once we have intellectualized the specific thing that we want to teach (whether this is a skill, an idea, a fact, a creative process, etc.), we can then move on to decide how we actually want to teach it. This might be by instructing and informing the children, or by encouraging them to discover it for themselves.

Instruction v. discovery

I hear and I forget. I see and I remember. I do and I understand.

Confucius

I have already talked at some length about the importance of finding a balance when we are being creative – about the delicate equilibrium between freedom and control that is inherent in any creative endeavour. If we are aiming to become more creative in our teaching, and to encourage that creative frame of mind in our students, then it is essential that we also achieve this balance within our classrooms.

Part of the balance for which we are searching will be between letting the children use their creative powers to discover things anew for themselves, and using our own knowledge to direct learning and pass on information. At various times during the history of education, one approach has been favoured over another. In recent years, the balance has tipped far more towards learning by instruction, towards the direct whole-class teaching of skills and techniques. With the current emphasis on thinking skills and creativity, however, it seems that we are due for a welcome change in direction. In any case, despite what is currently popular, the majority of teachers carry on using a sensible mixture of approaches to teach their classes.

Instruction and creativity

To a certain extent, we are wasting our children's time if we constantly make them re-invent the wheel. Not every theory, fact or idea that has been discovered or developed in the past needs to be rediscovered with every passing generation. Although open-ended questions and situations are great for learning creatively, there will be times when it is easier or more sensible to simply pass on the information that is needed. We cannot expect every single child to 'discover' every single thing about the world for him or herself.

However, when you do need to spend time instructing and informing your class, this can actually be done in a creative way. In these instances, although we are not 'teaching for creativity', i.e. using activities that encourage our children to develop their own creativity, we can certainly 'teach creatively' and encourage a creative spirit within our classrooms. The key seems to be in finding ways of making concepts concrete for the children, so that they get to 'do' the concept in a real and practical way.

Let me give you an example to clarify what I mean. Imagine for a moment that you are a primary school teacher about to teach basic division to your class for the very first time. There are various approaches that you might take, some more creative, imaginative and interesting than others. You could:

- Tell the class that $8 \div 4 = 2$.
- Write the sum on the board.
- Draw eight dots on the board and ask the students to divide them up into four equal amounts.
- Give each of the children eight bricks, asking them to split the bricks into four equal piles, then count how many bricks are in each pile.
- Get eight children to stand at the front of the class, then ask another child to come and split the group into four equal-sized groups, before counting how many children are in each group.
- Split the class up into groups of four. Give each group a

packed lunch box which has eight sandwiches in it. Ask the children to share the sandwiches out so that each person has an equal amount.

- Set up a teddy bears' picnic in the classroom. Tell the children a story about how Big Ted held a teddy bears' picnic for his birthday, illustrating the story with lots of props (teddies, picnic rug, etc.). 'Big Ted invited seven teddies to come to his party, and he cut his cake into eight slices so that each of his teddy friends could have one slice, and he could have one as well. Four of his friends got lost in the woods, so he was left with himself, his three friends and eight slices of cake. How can we divide up the cakes equally between the teddies?' A complicated scenario for explaining a simple concept, but one that will lend itself to looking at fractions as well, e.g. five teddies and three pieces of cake.

Discovery and creativity
Creative activity could be described as a type of learning process where teacher and pupil are located in the same individual.

Arthur Koestler

When a child sets out on a journey of creativity, the teacher will of necessity take a bit more of a back seat than when he or she is using an instructive approach. However, the teacher still has an important role to play, and this role might take a variety of different forms:

- Acting as an overall 'guide' during the journey, for instance gently nudging the children back onto the path if they get a bit lost.
- Sparking off the children's inspiration by offering a variety of unusual resources.
- Deciding on a specific form or medium for the work.
- Structuring the lesson to ensure focus and safety.
- Giving details about how particular techniques work, and offering some interesting ideas about using them.
- Passing on any information or background details that might be useful.

Finding ways to help our children 'discover' creative learning for themselves is not as simple as it might sound. Once again, we must walk backwards down that path to learning – intellectualizing the various steps that we ourselves took to discover or understand a particular concept or idea, or to develop a particular type of creative piece. After we have done this, we can then set up a situation in which the children are likely to work in a creative manner. The success of the work that takes place will depend on how effectively the teacher has set up the classroom situation. There are many factors that will play a part in this, including the provision of a wide range of resources, a good balance between structure and freedom, an environment that lends itself to the creative process, and so on.

In the next section ('Freedom v. security') I discuss some of the ways in which teachers might vary the set-up to ensure that a balance is maintained. It can be hard for teachers to let go of the reins and allow their children to learn via discovery as well as through instruction. However, we cannot impose or instruct the creative impulse in our children; we can only set it free and stand back to see where it takes them. Of course, our ultimate aim should be to set the children off on a journey that is entirely of their own making. And as we pat them on the back, wish them well, and watch them head off into the distance, we surely hope that they will leave us far behind in their eventual destination.

Freedom v. security

As well as achieving a balance between discovery and instruction, we also need to balance the creative, imaginative delivery and content of our lessons with the importance of maintaining a safe and secure learning environment. Just as with the creative process itself, inspiration and imagination must be balanced with suitable levels of structure and technique. We cannot simply set up a potentially creative situation or environment and then just let our children get on with it. Although this might work in some instances, on many occasions it will simply lead to total chaos. This is particularly so when you are working with a class who have not been given much free rein before, or with children who find it hard to control their own behaviour in less structured situations.

It is perhaps counter-intuitive, but creative activities actually require a very high level of classroom management skill – far more so than when we are simply giving instructions or passing on information. Of course we want our students to feel free enough to take risks and make mistakes, but children being children they will inevitably push at the boundaries of what is acceptable. There will always be the potential for the children to get over-excited or even completely out of control, and it is part of our role as professionals to manage this potential. Balancing freedom with security is tricky to get right. Your decisions about how much structure and how much freedom to allow will need to be based on the following factors:

- The prior experience this particular group of students has had of creative, loosely structured approaches.
- How well the children can manage their own behaviour and learning.
- The potential for any tricky individuals to lose self-control.
- How well you know the children and their likely reactions to the work.
- Your own current levels of skill in classroom and behaviour management.
- Your levels of experience in managing practical, freeform work.
- How many risks you personally feel comfortable about taking.
- The type of teaching space within which you are working. This can prove a real constraint when trying to incorporate movement-based activities.
- The impact on other classes working nearby.
- Management attitudes at your school about appropriate levels of noise and movement during lessons.

The teacher effectively has to 'police' or oversee the creative efforts to ensure that safety is maintained, and that good quality learning takes place. Depending on the class involved, this might mean simply being in a position to rein them in if the lesson looks like getting out of control, or it could mean using quite highly structured approaches to creative learning. Generally speaking:

- The more often you use creative approaches with your children, the better able both you and they will be to cope with the 'freedom' part of the equation, and the less structure and restraint you will need to incorporate.

- The more freedom and choice you can incorporate, the more likely your students are to be able to apply their creativity in a genuinely innovative and original way.
- The more your children decide on the directions of their own learning, the better chance there is of them creating something imaginative and original.

Some teachers are understandably nervous about using unstructured, creative work in their classrooms, perhaps because they don't have much experience of approaching learning in this way. At first, you might find that things don't go quite according to plan, and that some of your lessons do indeed descend into chaos. This is very much a learning experience, though, both in terms of your teaching skills and also in getting to know the students and the ways of working that best suit them. Try to keep your nerve and learn from what goes wrong. If you persevere, both you and your students will quickly become used to a more innovative and potentially far more interesting way of working.

Here are some tips and thoughts about incorporating more structure into freeform, creative activities.

- *Control it from the front*: If you feel at all nervous about trying out more creative approaches in your classroom, then start off by controlling the work from the front. For instance, in a history lesson you decide to set up a role-play. The children are going to play the characters of Ancient Egyptians, to explore the lives of these people. For the first lesson you bring in lots of beautiful Egyptian costumes borrowed from a local theatre group. You are understandably nervous about these getting damaged. At this point, if you have any concerns about how the children might react, then control the lesson from the front. Ask for some volunteers to come up and try the costumes on (those who are behaving impeccably, of course). The class can then discuss their initial reactions together. If at this stage you are impressed with their behaviour and responses, you might allow them to break up into small groups so that they all get a chance to try on the costumes.

- *Manage the level of choice*: Children can sometimes feel over-whelmed, or alternatively get very over-excited, when there are lots of options from which to choose. For example, a teacher might be doing some artwork based on the theme of the wind. With a class used to freeform, loosely structured work, you might set up different tables with different types of resources (paints, pencils, crayons, pastels, cardboard, clay, collage materials, etc.) and then allow the children free choice of the medium in which to work. In a class with less experience or with less self-control, it could be that you only offer one or two mediums (e.g. paint and clay) with which the children can work.

- *Include preparation time*: When setting up a creative activity, you can mitigate against the problems caused by too much freedom by including lots of preparation time before the main, creative event. By giving the children the 'carrot' of a lesson with lots of freedom and experimentation, you can ensure that they take the preparation work seriously. For example, imagine you are planning to do a lesson called 'The French Market', in which the students set up and run stalls and go shopping at a market in France. Before the lesson in which the market takes place, you could get the class to spend time planning the different stalls, gathering resources, learning the appropriate French vocabulary, and so on. By the time they get to the less structured part of the work, they will have all their preparation in place and this will give them and you a greater feeling of security.

- *Incorporate structures and restrictions*: The teacher can include various restrictions within the lesson delivery to ensure that the work remains structured and controlled. This might mean giving the class a limited time period in which to complete each section of the creative activity, for instance, five minutes to do an initial brainstorm. In fact, having short, sharp targets for which to aim will often help the children to retain their focus and stay on task. The best creativity will not necessarily come about as a result of having endless quantities of time.

- *Use the fun to control the class*: When it comes to managing behaviour, one of the most powerful incentives of all is the chance to do what is seen as 'fun' work. Use this to develop a powerful partnership with your children. Explain to them that if they would like you to take more creative approaches, and to do lots of fun and creative activities, then they must prove to you that they can control themselves.

- *Motivation and trust lead to self-discipline*: It can be tempting not to use these more creative, imaginative approaches to teaching with particularly difficult classes. When we are working with children who seem to have a total lack of self-discipline, we might decide not to take the risk of seeing what will happen if we give them a bit of freedom. However, my own experience of working with these types of classes actually suggests the opposite: that, if you can bring yourself to give these children the necessary trust, they will often demonstrate amazingly high levels of self-motivation and self-control. This will not necessarily hold true every time – but we must be willing to take the risks if we want to have any chance of getting the results.

- *Practice makes perfect*: The more often you use these creative approaches with your children, the easier you will find it to control what goes on. This is partly because you will be developing aspects of your classroom management technique; it will also be because the children come to know what you expect from them. At first, you might find that they try to push it, getting over-excited or running around the room. Eventually, though, they will come to understand and enjoy this more innovative way of working.

To better explain how the ideas and strategies given above might work, I'd like to look at the opening of one topic that I've used in my own classroom. Below you will find two possible ways of delivering the same topic, which demonstrate the different levels of structure that might be used. This is part of a series of lessons designed to explore the topic of 'communication' with drama students.

The work is based around the idea that the class are a tribe of Native American Indians. The objective of the lessons is that they will find ways of communicating across the barriers of location and language. The creative journey undertaken in this series of lessons is very much a group endeavour – developing and exploring as a whole class within the tribal 'group'.

The highly structured approach

Before beginning the drama activity, the teacher gives the class various research materials so that they can gather lots of information about Native American Indians. She starts the next lesson by asking the class to sit in a circle on the floor. She tells the students that they will be acting as Native Americans in the next few lessons. The teacher leads the class in a discussion of the various roles and activities that might take place within a tribe. The teacher then structures and leads an in-role discussion with the tribal group.

The freeform approach

As soon as the class arrive at the room, the teacher goes into character. She is holding a feathered 'talking stick' and she addresses them using the role of the Chieftain. 'Welcome to our tribal meeting,' she begins, 'please come and sit in our traditional circle on the floor. As you know, this is the last time you will see me for many moons. The time has come to find a new place for us to camp, and I must go ahead into the wilderness to begin the search. When I find our new camp, I will send word so that you can come and join me.'

At this point, the teacher might choose to add a small amount of structure, by saying to the class, 'While I am gone, you must elect a new Chieftain.' She could also set up an activity by saying, 'You will need to pack up the camp and make ready to leave this place' or 'While I am gone, remember to do our tribal dance once a day.' Alternatively, she might just 'leave' in character, and then step back to see what happens next. When using these in-role activities in my own classroom, I have found that at first the children are a bit stumped about what to do next. It is never long, though, before one of the students gets the idea and the work starts to take shape.

Teaching styles and creativity

Every teacher will have his or her own, unique 'style' of teaching. In fact, in some ways our teaching style will be a creative endeavour in itself – a work in progress that has developed over many years! Our teaching style will be influenced by many different factors, including:

- The way we use our voices, facial expressions and body language.
- The way we use space and levels within our teaching spaces.
- The content and delivery of our lessons.
- Our appearance – what we wear and also what we look like.
- Our personality and attitudes to life, whether positive or negative.
- How much experience we have, both of teaching and also in the world beyond school.
- The type of children we are teaching.
- The ethos of the school where we work.

Some teaching styles will inevitably lend themselves better to creativity than others. Once again, it is about finding a balance between freedom and structure. It goes without saying that if you rule your class by fear, you can hardly expect your students to be fearless and to take risks. Similarly, if you are totally disorganized in preparing for your lessons, then there may well be more chaos than creativity in your classroom. If our aim is to encourage and develop our students' creativity, it is well worth thinking about ways in which we can adapt our own teaching style to better facilitate this process. For instance, you might consider:

- Playing around with the way that you use your voice – adding in some accents or using an exaggerated tone to get your class excited about a topic.
- Adapting the way that you use the space – teaching from the back of the room rather than from the front for a change.
- Working with some different levels – sitting or standing on a chair or table, or getting your students to sit on their desks or on the floor for an informal discussion session.
- Taking some risks with your planning, and experimenting with leaving things to chance, especially if you normally tend to stick to highly structured lessons.
- Wearing a completely different style of outfit to school, or even dressing up in a costume.

5 The creative lesson

We'll teach you to drink deep ere you depart.

William Shakespeare

When writing about teaching, I have often drawn parallels between teachers and actors. In the classroom, we take on a teacher 'character' which is at least partially divorced from our own selves outside of the learning environment. For instance, we might put on a bit of a 'strict and scary' persona to help us control a class of riotous youngsters. Taking this metaphor to its logical conclusion, the lessons that we teach are effectively performances, with the children playing their own roles in the show. They might simply be an audience if we are instructing them, or they might take a more active role as participants when the learning is discovery based. And the more interesting and imaginative our performance is, the more creative our lesson will be.

In this chapter I discuss what is actually meant by a creative lesson. I look at how we can plan lessons that will help develop our children's creativity, and the type of approaches that we might usefully adopt. I examine some of the ways in which we can get our students inspired, and how we can move on from this inspiration to help them structure their ideas in the most effective ways. I give some ideas for warm-ups and creative starters that could be incorporated into your lessons. Finally, I look at how you can create fictional simulations to encourage and develop creativity in your classroom.

What is a creative lesson?

Spoon feeding in the long run teaches us nothing but the shape of the spoon.

E. M. Forster

The most obvious answer to the question 'what is a creative lesson?' might seem to be either (a) one that is likely to encourage our children to develop their creativity, or (b) one which is delivered in a creative manner. Of course, a lesson in which the teacher stands at the front and delivers facts is unlikely to encourage much in the way of creative contributions from the children. Similarly, a lesson in which the teacher hands out a worksheet with a 'fill in the blanks' style exercise on it is not really going to stretch our students in their creative thinking. In brief, a creative lesson is one in which the children and teacher employ or develop the creative frame of mind described in this book (see pp. 46–8 and pp. 58–61).

Clearly, some areas of the curriculum will lend themselves naturally to the use of creative approaches. Creativity is of course at the very heart of what goes on in an art, music or drama lesson. In these subjects, though, there is still the possibility that creativity can be stifled rather than developed. In an art lesson where the children are asked to copy a painting of a forest, they will not develop anything original or imaginative. On the other hand, imagine an art lesson where the children are given a range of resources – sticks, twigs, soil, leaves, seeds, straw, etc. – and asked to spend some time feeling, looking at, and talking about them. They then move on to brainstorm some rough initial impressions around 'the forest' on a big sheet of paper. All the while, a tape of forest sounds is playing in the background. Once the children have their initial set of images and ideas, they move on to choose a medium within which to work, developing their own images inspired by all these different stimuli.

If you are teaching a subject not traditionally thought of as 'creative' (science, maths, RE, geography, and so on) you might find it a bit harder to think of ways of developing creativity in your lessons. We might assume that to do this we simply need to incorporate aspects from the performing arts, e.g. how can I include a bit of music in this geography lesson? Of course, there is no harm at all in doing this, and it may well enhance our children's creative responses, but it is not necessarily going to get them thinking and acting creatively in respect of that subject. Creativity is not just about producing the kind of artwork described above; it is also about applying lateral thinking to solve problems, or asking unusual questions that bring up an interesting range of possible answers.

In recent years teachers have been increasingly encouraged to see the curriculum as being divided up into different subjects, and beyond that into individual skills and techniques. At primary level, the literacy and numeracy strategies take up increasing amounts of time, often to the detriment of other subjects. At secondary level, the subjects are already set apart by their division into departments or faculties. If we hope to encourage creativity, though, we need to do exactly the opposite – find connections and links, rather than make divisions. So, a creative lesson might also aim to find and utilize these connecting strands between different subjects.

Planning for creativity

Because of the random nature of the creative impulse, the notion of planning for creativity is essentially a bit of a paradox. When we plan out a lesson in minute detail, this leaves very little room for the flexibility and freedom that play such a key part in the creative journey. In other words, planning can actually mitigate *against* creativity, rather than encourage it!

However, what we can do is to plan lessons that have the *potential* to develop our children's creativity, while at the same time ensuring that our planning does not set too much in stone. The planning that we do should allow for that element of creativity whereby we follow random leads when they occur. Rather than feeling the need to map out every moment of every lesson for our students, we need to teach ourselves to follow our children's leads as well.

Speaking at a very personal level, some of the most creative lessons that I have taught have been those for which I did the least planning – where I have entered the room with only the vaguest of notions about what would happen during the lesson, perhaps clutching a single inspirational resource in my hand. None of this will endear me to Ofsted inspectors or PGCE tutors, but it's my belief that this kind of risk taking has made me a better, more interesting, and more effective teacher, and that it has enhanced the creativity of the children that I've taught.

Of course, I do accept that lesson planning is an important elem-ent of the work that we do. There will be many occasions where we need to take a reasonably structured approach to lessons, so that we cover the relevant material. Planning out the potential journey of each lesson will help us ensure that we achieve those ever present 'learning objectives'. When we first start out as teachers, having clear lesson plans gives us the confidence that we need to progress through a lesson. With all this in mind, here are some practical tips and ideas about how you can plan for creativity.

- *Encourage a creative frame of mind*: Inspire your children to approach every moment of the school day in a creative way. Look for creative ways of doing the most mundane of tasks (perhaps using some of the ideas suggested in Chapter 4, pp. 61–5). Try to constantly involve your children in finding creative new ideas about how your lessons might progress.
- *Don't re-invent the wheel*: Have a look through the lesson plans and schemes of work that you already have in your school or department. There are likely to be plenty of opportunities in these for encouraging more creative responses from your children, so adapt what is already there rather than feeling that you need to start from scratch.
- *Think about timing*: Creativity typically takes time to achieve, and it could be that you need to devote a series of lessons to one creative activity, although I'm aware that this might be difficult within the constraints of the curriculum. Conversely, some really good creative work can be done in very short bursts, with a high level of focus from the children.
- *Intellectualize the process*: Talk to the class about the type of steps, stages or techniques that might be used. A very good way to do this is to produce a similar piece yourself, and then work backwards through your own intellectual processes, as outlined in the previous chapter (see pp. 66–8).
- *Show them the possibilities*: Explain the likely outcomes of the creative work you are doing, and perhaps share some examples with the children. However, you will need to be careful that they don't simply end up copying what they have already seen.
- *Encourage participation*: Find ways of involving your children in what they do and how they do it, rather than seeing your lessons as a 'command down' process. Don't always feel the need to tell the children how to approach the work. Aim to

incorporate at least some opportunities for them to make their own choices and indeed mistakes.

- *Keep the outcomes in mind*: Consider the outcome that you might like to see, e.g. 'we'll all end up with a finished painting', but don't be afraid to let this slip if it seems likely to undermine creativity. Talk with the children about the outcomes that you and they hope might result from their work. This will help keep them on task and sustain their focus.

- *Incorporate feedback sessions*: As the creative product takes shape, it can be very helpful for children to have feedback on their work so far. This might mean stopping the class to share the work that has been done up to that point. Try to ensure that this feedback is either positive or, if critical, makes constructive suggestions for further improvement.

- *Appeal to a range of 'learning styles'*: The teacher who includes a range of approaches in his or her lesson will inevitably appeal to children who learn best in different ways. This might mean using a variety of resources – images, music, props. It could mean using a range of approaches – practical work, writing, drawing, and so on.

- *Experiment with constraint and control*: Sometimes, setting very clear and constrained activities will help your children to channel their creativity. You might set short targets (e.g. 'brainstorm ten words') or brief time limits (e.g. 'do it in two minutes'). Experiment to see which restrictions help your children to work more creatively, and which ones simply dampen their imagination.

- *Experiment with abandon and freedom*: Similarly, you can encourage your children to practise the 'freedom' part of the equation, by setting them tasks that are much more open ended. This might involve word associations, free choice of form or materials, streams of consciousness (see p. 89), and so on.

- *Find 'real' audiences*: If we can make the creative process as 'real' as possible, then this will help us motivate our children in striving to produce their best. It will also help make the creativity feel natural rather than forced. There are plenty of options for finding real audiences, including other children in the class or school, parents, on the internet, local papers, magazines, and so on.

- *Give a range of experiences*: The wider the range of previous experiences we have, the greater the well of ideas on which we can draw. Offer your children the whole gamut of potential experiences, such as visits or trips, artists in residence, etc.

- *Find inspirational starting points*: Starting your lessons with a 'bang' will ensure that, at the very least, you have your children's attention. Using an inspirational starting point will help them head off on the creative journey. This might mean using props, stories, events, questions – whatever you can find. When you do present your class with some resources for inspiration, try to offer them the widest possible range of choice. That way they will hopefully find something that really appeals to them and sparks their thinking.

- *Make it relevant and topical*: School can seem a rather artificial environment, removed from our children's experiences of everyday life. Find ways to bring the outside world into your teaching, for instance by making reference to topical events from the news, or by focusing on your students' favourite hobbies. You might use the simulations described on pp. 93–102 to create a small slice of 'real life' in your classroom.

- *Take time to talk*: It can sometimes feel as though we have very little time to just kick back and have a chat in our classrooms. This is a real shame, because talking can bring up some really useful creative material, as well as being very positive and beneficial in its own right. We might talk with our students about their own personal experiences, their feelings and emotions, their intuitive responses, their daydreams or hopes for the future. In the primary classroom, the teacher might set aside some time each day or week for the whole class to have a chat about what they've been up to. In the secondary school, the form tutor is the person most likely to be able to find the time required to do this.

- *Don't be afraid to go off at a tangent*: Sometimes a child will bring up a fascinating idea or an unusual question that takes you away from your original lesson objectives. This is where excessive structure can let us down – we are too tempted to stick to what we had planned rather than to 'go with the flow'. When you're offered a good lead from your class, grasp it with both hands and take a risk – it might lead you nowhere, but you could well be surprised at what comes next.

Approaches for creativity

People rarely succeed unless they have fun in what they are doing.

Dale Carnegie

First and foremost, if we're going to be creative, we need to be allowed to *play*. It's only by playing around with ideas, images, words, numbers, or whatever the medium is, that we can hope to come up with an innovative and imaginative result. In the very early years of schooling (in the nursery or reception class), play is seen as a wonderful tool in helping our children to learn. Few would argue that young children are not learning as they dig in the sand and build sandcastles, or as they experiment with pouring water from one container to another. At some point in primary school, though, 'play' starts to be seen as a dirty word – one that must be replaced by the more adult 'work'.

The intuitive mind is a sacred gift, and the rational mind a faithful servant. We have created a society that honours the servant and has forgotten the gift.

Albert Einstein

Of course, our children do need to be taught techniques, and these will not transmit themselves by osmosis. It is certainly important to teach our children the skills of literacy, numeracy, scientific experimentation, and so on (although hopefully to teach them in a creative way). However, when it comes to encouraging each child's creative potential, these techniques and skills are only ever a means to an end. If we hope to develop a society full of innovation and creativity, rather than one that consists only of 'worker bees', then it is essential that we rediscover a balance between skills and creativity.

If we are genuinely going to encourage creativity, then we must make proper space and time for our students of whatever age to play with ideas, materials, sounds, questions, and so on. A change in mindset will need to occur – it cannot be seen as simply an 'add on' to the teaching of facts and techniques. Instead, we must encourage the creative frame of mind discussed previously every day, hour, minute, second of the school day.

Here are some suggestions for approaches that will encourage this creative mindset among your students.

- Role-plays, fictional scenarios and simulations, as described on pp. 93–102.
- A wide range of resources – letting the children respond to them and use them as they wish.
- Concentration and meditative exercises, as described on p. 30.
- Random words, pictures, sounds, etc. to inspire creativity.
- Seeing the 'flip side' – looking at the reverse of an issue, seeing things backwards.
- Looking for what is not rather than what is.
- Using all the senses, and building the 'creative senses' described above.

In praise of topic work

Although it has fallen out of favour in recent years, project or topic work does tend to lead more naturally to creative approaches and responses. It offers us a way of capitalizing on the natural links and connections between various subjects. It also allows our children to follow their impulses where they lead, rather than always feeling that the teacher must dictate the progress and direction of the learning.

Topic work offers a good way of starting a creative journey – we might use a single starting point as our inspiration (the senses, butterflies, mini beasts, fireworks) and move on to develop work in many different curriculum areas. Although topic work is perhaps more easily incorporated at primary school level, there is certainly the potential for secondary teachers from different subject areas to work together around a similar starting point.

Finding inspiration

Inspiration can basically come from absolutely anything at all. If you stop reading this book for a moment and look around you, you will see a whole range of things that are potential sources of inspiration. As well as coming from an external source, inspiration can also come from within – the question that puzzles us, the thought that suddenly occurs. Finding inspiration is not only an issue in the arts subjects – we would surely hope to inspire our children in every area of the curriculum.

Inspiration often acts as a leap-pad into creative thinking or into the imagination – as a way of getting the ideas flooding in. Sometimes the progress of the creative journey will stick very closely to that initial starting point; at other times it will deviate from it totally. The inspiration is not an end in itself, it is just a way of getting started. To find inspiration for and with your children you might:

- Search the 'database' inside your brain for a thought, image, experience, etc. that offers an interesting direction.
- Look around yourself for inspiration – the physical environment, other people, snippets of conversation, and so on.
- Use your senses to find interesting or unusual responses. We typically focus on sight and hearing, but try focusing on your other senses instead. A helpful way of doing this is to cut off a sense, for instance by using a blindfold.

When offering your children some form of inspiration, you are essentially giving them a stimulus to get their creative thinking going. Here are some possibilities for inspiring your children, which might be used right across the curriculum.

- *Natural materials and 'found' objects*: sand, water, soil, mud, shells, rocks and pebbles, leaves, plants (including herbs and flowers), feathers, conkers.
- *Manmade objects*: tiles, bricks, clothing, hats, bottles, containers, wheels, keys, bags, coins, cards.
- *Images*: photographs, postcards, paintings, graffiti, CD covers, newspapers, magazines, maps, food packaging, computers, television, looking out of the window.
- *Sounds*: music (classical, modern and popular), percussive noises (cymbals, drums, etc.), noises made by different materials, vocal sounds, noises around the school.
- *Words*: single words, phrases, quotations, pieces of writing, stories, 'taking a word for a walk'.

When choosing inspiration, the teacher will have to make some decisions about how this will be done. You might:

- Offer the whole class the same starting point (a piece of music, a word, an image).
- Ask the children to choose from a variety of inspirations in the same medium (a series of postcards, a range of different shells).
- Give the students a free choice of inspirations from a range of resources that you offer them.
- Ask the children to bring in an inspirational starting point of their own.

Working with ideas

Once your children have found or been given that initial stimulus, that source of inspiration, the next step is to get them actually building and structuring the ideas that arise out of the starting point. This will take them into the 'improvisation' stage of the creative journey discussed in Chapter 2 (pp. 26–7). There are two main approaches that might be taken:

- *Close observation*: You might give the class some time in which to simply observe, study or think about an object, idea or question. During this time, encourage them to respond to the stimulus with all their different senses.
- *Dive straight in*: Alternatively, you could get the children to plunge straight into talking about or noting down their ideas in some way. This might be via one of the structures that I have given below.

If your children are used to jumping straight to an end product, it might take them some time to get used to the notion of just scribbling down ideas. At the initial improvisation stage, keep reminding your class that there is no right or wrong answer (indeed, there is often no particular answer at all). When writing down and working with ideas, I often tell my students not to worry about spelling and other aspects of technique. This helps free them up to concentrate on content over presentation.

Structures for improvisation

There are various key structures for working with ideas. Most teachers will be very familiar with the brainstorm as a way of starting off a topic. Brainstorms are useful in that they help your children to note down initial ideas and impressions, and also because they allow the teacher to find out what the children already know or feel about a subject. Brainstorms might be used as a whole-class activity, with the teacher noting down the children's ideas on the board, or as an individual, paired or small group activity. Brainstorms are very much the baby brother of the mind-map which I discuss in some detail below.

As well as using brainstorms, there are some other very useful ways of getting your children to develop and work with their ideas. These include:

- *Free associations*: Start with a single word or image and get the class to come up with associations or links from this point. This might be done by asking the children to give single words around a circle, or by writing down all the words that occur to them.
- *Collages*: When the teacher intends the class to work from a more visual point of view, making collages is a great way of developing and structuring ideas. Give the children a range of magazines, some scissors and some glue and get them to create visual maps of their thinking.
- *Stream of consciousness*: This is an excellent way of finding and working with ideas. After getting an initial stimulus (a word, an image), give the children a very brief period in which to respond. When you say 'go', ask them to start writing and not to pause until you say 'stop'. They should aim not to let the pen stop moving. Tell them not to worry about spelling or punctuation – the intention is simply to empty all the contents of their minds onto the paper. If they get stuck during the stream of consciousness, they should simply write the same word over and over until they get unstuck. At the end of the time, you might get the children to narrow down the results by highlighting only the most interesting ideas for further investigation.

Using mind-maps

There will often be reasonably little difficulty for the teacher in getting the children to produce a vast quantity of ideas or associations. However, one of the key skills in moving from this explosion of ideas to a finished and creative 'end product' is the ability to both structure and edit down all this material.

One of the very best ways of putting a structure on our ideas is to use a mind-map. This is literally a 'map' of the different thoughts that are going on in our brains. Mind-maps were first created in the 1960s by Tony Buzan, and you can find lots of further detail about them (including some useful examples) at his website: www.mind-map. com.

Mind-maps offer an excellent way of working with ideas because:

- They let you organize the material into different areas.
- They allow you to find links between one area or idea and another.
- They give you an 'overview' of the subject, topic or idea as a whole.
- They emulate the way that the mind works – structuring and finding relationships between different points or ideas.
- Further, and often more unusual, ideas may occur to the person during the course of putting the material down on the page.

Here are some thoughts about making the best use of mind-maps.

- *Give it sufficient space*: Although at first glance your initial ideas might seem few in number, once you start to map them out you may realize that there is tons of material to include. Of course, space may be an issue for you, and you will need to be creative in working with what you have available. You might give each child a large sheet of paper, and then find an open space such as the school hall in which to work. You could get the children working in groups, with one large sheet of paper on each table. Alternatively, why not get the whole class working in tandem to create a giant, classroom-sized mind-map?
- *Use diagrams, symbols and images*: Mind-maps are not necessarily just about words. Using diagrams, symbols and images can offer a shorthand for our thinking processes. You might be

using arrows to link ideas together, question marks to suggest an area that needs further thought, thought bubbles to enclose unusual ideas that occur to you, double underlining for key points, and so on. In a mind-map for a piece of artwork, the entire piece might be a series of images, textures, colours, materials, and so on, gathered from lots of different sources.

- *Use colour, shape and size*: These can be incorporated to show the differences between areas of thinking, and also to demonstrate links between different ideas. For instance, in a mind-map based on the title 'The Elements', you might use blue to indicate water, brown for Earth, and so on. When an interesting thought occurs that you'd like to return to, this might be written down in a large thought bubble. Similarly, you might write down the more important thoughts or ideas in a larger size handwriting.

- *See it as a work in progress*: Mind-maps are best viewed as a draft in continual progress, rather than as anything that will ever be presented as a finished product. This is a 'map' of what is going on in your mind, and does not need to relate visually to the final piece in any way whatsoever. No one ever need see it, if you do not want to share it with others. If and when you do get to the stage of a final product, it can be very interesting to look back at your mind-map to see the links and connections between the two.

Warm-ups for creativity

Preparing for a 'bout' of creativity means getting ready for what can be both a mentally and a physically taxing activity. We would think nothing of warming up for a physically active lesson – a game of football or a dance class. However, we do seem to shy away from physical and mental warm-ups when we are doing classroom-based tasks. This is a shame: these warm-ups can be great fun, and they also play a useful part in getting our children in the right mental and physical state for creative work.

When they arrive at the classroom, our children's minds will often be full of 'baggage' that comes from outside the classroom or, often, outside the school itself. This baggage (a fight at break time, a quarrel with parents) might get in the way of the creative impulse.

There are literally too many bits and pieces going around in their brains for them to focus on the creative activity at hand. Some artists will describe how they go into a focused state of mind when being creative: almost as though nothing exists between the person and the 'thing' that is being created. Our aim should be to encourage our children to get as close to this totally focused state as they can.

Below you will find lots of ideas for both physical and mental warm-ups that you can use in a classroom, a school hall or even in the playground. Although some of these warm-ups might seem best suited for drama lessons, in fact they can play a part in loosening up your children's imaginations whatever the subject. For instance, you might be planning to look at the experiences of soldiers going to war in a history lesson. In this case, you could start off the lesson by asking the children to move around the space as though they are fearful of what lies ahead. Later on during the lesson you might talk about their emotional responses and reactions during this warm-up activity, and link these to the feelings of soldiers going off to war.

Physical warm-ups
- Moving around the room in different ways:
  - With an emotion: tired, happy, excited, nervous, terrified
  - With a character: a solider on duty, an old lady, a young child
  - With a location: through a hot desert, across thin ice, through a tangled forest
  - With the imagination: over a sleeping monster's back, through the clouds
  - With a material: through glue, over nails, across broken glass.
- Working in small groups to form shapes with their bodies of:
  - A moving machine
  - A number
  - A letter
  - A word
  - An animal.
- Warming up the hands by:
  - Clenching their fingers into fists, then stretching them out

- Shaking their fingers in the air
- Clicking or clapping.
- Running and freezing in position as:
  - An animal
  - An emotion
  - A shape
  - A symbol.

Mental warm-ups

- Closing their eyes and simply listening for 2 to 3 minutes to see what sounds they can hear in the classroom and beyond.
- Spelling various words backwards in their heads (perhaps relating to the subject or topic of the lesson).
- Meditative activities, such as those described on p. 30.

Using simulations

When in doubt, make a fool of yourself. There is a microscopically thin line between being brilliantly creative and acting like the most gigantic idiot on Earth. So what the hell, leap.

Cynthia Heimel

One very powerful way of harnessing and developing creativity is to set up simulated experiences or situations in the classroom. These simulations are intended to replicate 'real' scenarios from the world outside of school (although often set in an entirely different time period, field of work or location to the norm). At secondary level, simulations can be used in a whole variety of different subject areas; at primary level, they can be used as a method of linking up various subjects under a cross-curricular umbrella. In many ways, they are the logical extension of the role-play areas that many primary school teachers already have in their classrooms.

This approach is very much one born out of the drama class-room. However, it is such a powerful technique that it can usefully be incorporated into lessons in any subject at all. Because they arise out of characterization, simulations work especially well in subjects that involve the study of people – history, geography, PSHE, citizenship. However, the possibilities for using this technique are endless – the only limits are those imposed by (a) the curriculum and (b) your imagination! Simulations can encourage some very highly creative approaches and attitudes in your children.

Far too many children, it seems, are almost totally de-motivated and switched off by their experience of school. It seems to bear little relation to the reality of their lives outside of the school buildings. Those of us who have had the luxury of a comfortable background might find it hard to understand, but for some of our students the world of the streets seems far more real and relevant than that of the classroom. The closer to 'real life' that we can get in our classrooms, the more motivated and engaged our children will be. This is where simulations come in.

One of the key attributes of simulations is that they come at a subject or topic from the widest of overviews – from how they would be applicable to real life, rather than by the teaching of individual facts, skills or techniques. So it is that, instead of spending a lesson or two teaching your class specifically how to 'identify, select and use a range of appropriate sources of information' (from the English History National Curriculum for Key Stage 3), you could instead set up a situation in which this skill, and many others, will be used as a natural part of the scenario.

At first, it might feel a little odd for you to be using a fictional approach in your lessons, particularly if you have not done so before. You could feel a bit daft taking on a character in front of your children (creativity often feels a bit embarrassing!). You might also be a bit concerned about how your students will react, and whether you will be able to control their responses.

Try not to worry, though. Once the simulation begins, the children should very quickly dive headfirst into the scenario, taking responsibility for their own work and behaviour because they are playing 'grown up' people. If you are still concerned, it might help you to know that this type of work has been most successful for me with my most difficult classes and my most 'challenging' students.

There are many potential benefits in using simulations for at least some of the work that you do in your classroom. These benefits include the following:

- The simulation becomes a kind of whole-class creative journey – the group is working as one and applying their different skills and talents to generating a unique and creative storyline.

- Taking on another character, and moving with that character through some of life's experiences, will help bring out your children's creative powers, by harnessing and encouraging:
  - the power of their imaginations
  - empathy and insight into other people's lives
  - 'real-life' problem solving
  - a questioning and curious mind
  - the ability to see connections between different people, times and places
  - an open-minded exploration of various viewpoints
  - a sense of play and fun.
- Children love stories, and by taking part in a collective class story, they build strong bonds and can create some very powerful pieces of work. Bear in mind that the stories that are developed during a simulation are creative products in their own right: although they cannot be 'saved' or 'assessed', much of the power of the work will be in the way that it changes or develops your children's thinking.
- Almost as soon as they take on their new characters, the children seem to shed their old selves. They will often apply a maturity beyond their actual chronological years, extending the work well past what you might have anticipated or expected.
- Some children will amaze you by getting totally caught up in the fiction, and throwing in incredibly creative suggestions which sweep the class along as one.
- Because the children are enjoying the work, their sense of self-motivation and engagement are typically very high, and they work with enthusiasm and commitment.
- If the children drift off task, the teacher can regain their focus by talking about how these characters would behave in 'real life'.
- The children will learn creatively in various ways during a simulation:
  - Through the investigation and thought processes required for playing the characters or understanding a particular situation.
  - Through finding solutions to the problems that the teacher, or the situation, throws in their path.

- By creative discovery through actually 'living' the part.
- Through any specifically creative exercises that the teacher inputs into the work.

- The children find these types of exercises very memorable and enjoyable: behaviour tends to be excellent, and the learning of high quality. The teacher who uses this kind of work will typically generate an excellent reputation within the school.
- The 'real-life' nature of taking part in a simulation means that the students see that the work they are doing is applicable to the world beyond school.
- You can use simulations in a whole host of different subjects (in fact, in any curriculum area). This approach also offers an excellent way of combining work from several different subject areas, as you'll hopefully see from the example given below.
- These simulations offer a great way of incorporating the learning of lots of different skills, techniques, facts and concepts under one umbrella.

When working within a simulation, the children take on a character and literally 'experience' that person's work or life at first hand, harnessing their creativity to make decisions, examine experiences, and to create as realistic a simulated world as they can.

Before we look at some specific examples of simulations that might be used in the classroom, I'd like to give you some thoughts and tips on the management of this type of drama work. The advice given below covers the preparations that you might make before the lessons begin, and also some of the issues involved in actually managing the simulation as it progresses.

- *Decide on a scenario*: This will depend on the topic involved: sometimes a very obvious simulation will occur to you, although it is worth thinking laterally to see if a more unusual idea comes up; with other topics it will take a bit more thought. Your scenarios might arise out of:
  - A job or area of professional expertise: lab technician, soldier.
  - A time period: Victorian England, Ancient Rome.
  - A setting: the rainforest, the snowy wastes of the Arctic.

- A problem: trapped underground, on a runaway train.
- A fictional setting/character: fairytales, princes, wicked witch.
- A format from the television: chat shows, news programmes.
- A combination of some or all of the above: some villagers in Britain during the time of the Viking settlements are faced with a problem over a poisoned water supply.

- *Do your research*: Depending on your existing levels of knowledge about a particular place, time, location or set of characters, you might need to do some background research before you begin. This research can be incorporated into the investigations undertaken by your students during the simulation. It also makes a great homework task. The children who want to take the work one step further can really extend themselves outside of school.

- *Gather your resources*: Having props and costumes will add a level of realism to your simulation, and will help the children take it more seriously. There is something rather magical about seeing unusual items in the classroom, and these will quickly suck the students into your simulation, helping it become a more authentic experience.

- *Find a 'hook'*: In many instances, the teacher can begin the simulation by using a 'hook' to pull the children in. A letter might arrive, inviting the class to work as scientists at a top secret government laboratory; the class might dig up a treasure trove with some ancient artefacts from Roman times; the teacher could turn up at the first lesson dressed in character as a Victorian school mistress.

- *Find ways of adding tension*: All the best stories will have plenty of tension – a tricky problem that needs solving urgently, or an obstacle that stands in the characters' way. As you consider the potential of your scenario, look for ways in which you can add some difficulties for the children to deal with. This will help expand their creative thinking to the maximum.

- *Don't plan in too much detail*: Although you need to have some sense of where you're going, and the type of creative and learning activities that will happen in the lessons, try not to make too many decisions in advance. Once you get started, you will often find that the children lead the learning for themselves, or that great new ideas occur to you as the class build the story.

- *Guide the children into creative and lateral thinking*: Although the teacher should stay responsive to the direction in which the children take the lesson, he or she can play a key part in encouraging creative thinking. For instance, the students might be posed a question and plump immediately for the most obvious answer. The teacher can help them to extend and widen their thinking by intervening to insist on further discussion. Alternatively, he or she might throw a problem in the way of that obvious answer ('we can't do that, it's too dangerous'), to force the children to think laterally.

- *Think about timing*: On some occasions, you will not want to spend too much time on your simulation, and a single lesson will suffice. For instance, you might be using a chat show format to explore a topic such as teenage pregnancy. In other instances, the topic will take much longer to evolve and you might need to spend far more time on it. Sometimes the very briefest of simulations can be used to inspire thinking about a topic. For example, I once saw a history teacher start his lesson by passing around an empty jar and telling the students not to open it (which of course they did). By the end of the lesson (on the bubonic plague), the class had established that there was an infected flea in the jar. At this point they realized that it might not have been such a good idea to disobey sir.

- *Consider playing a part yourself*: It can work very well for the teacher to play an active part in the simulation. You might introduce the scenario in role (see below), and then play this character throughout the time that the class spend in working on the project, perhaps stepping in and out of the action as appropriate. Playing a part will allow you to direct the learning from inside the story that is created, controlling the scenario while remaining in character.

- *You don't have to explain the fiction*: A really good way of introducing a simulation is to go straight into character, rather than explaining what the lesson is going to be about. At first, you may find that your students are a bit confused and that they ask you 'Sir/Miss, what's going on?' Instead of going back into teacher mode, hold your nerve, continue to play your role and the children will soon pick up on what is happening.

- *Make use of special effects*: As well as using props as discussed above, it can be a great idea to include other dramatic effects, as this will help to engage the class and pull them into the story. You might use a tape of bird song to create a background atmosphere when working as explorers in the rainforest. You could give the children torches and darken the room if the simulation takes place in an underground cave.
- *Incorporate structure*: As we've seen, one of the keys to successful creativity is to balance freedom with structure. Using a simulation does not mean that you give the children characters to play and then just stand back to see what happens. This will often, although not always, result in chaos. The teacher can incorporate structure in various ways. You might:
  - Have a set list of tasks for the characters to complete.
  - Hold a meeting so that the children can discuss what needs to be done.
  - Use a series of interventions to move the story in a particular direction.
  - Set time limits for each part of the story.
- *Use the fun to control the class*: Students of any age will find simulations great fun. Use this to your advantage and it will help you control the situation. If the children do start getting over-excited you might:
  - Stay in character and refocus the group from inside the story.
  - Stop the simulation and explain to the class that they need to demonstrate self-discipline if they wish to continue with the work.

There are various techniques and approaches that can be used within simulations both to focus your children and to deepen their experience.

- *Whole-class meetings*: These might be used to discuss the progress and direction of the work, to take key decisions as a group, to develop the sense of character and period.
- *Small group work*: At various points during the course of the simulation, you might wish to break the class up into smaller

groups. These groups could be dictated by characters (e.g. 'all the carpenters get together and discuss how to solve this problem'), by family groups, or by any other link that you care to create.

- *Small group improvisations*: These might involve asking the students to summarize one small part of the story in a performance to the class. These could be completely improvised (made up as they go along) or a planned improvisation (discussed and practised beforehand).

- *Freeze frames*: It can be useful to summarize a moment by asking the children to create a frozen picture. This could be to explain more about their character ('I'm an unhappy washerwoman'), or perhaps to encapsulate a particular point in the story ('this happened during our journey into the wilderness').

- *Whole-class improvisations*: Of all the techniques, this is perhaps the most powerful, as it involves the whole class making up the story together with little if any prior decision making about what will happen. These improvisations will sometimes arise out of nowhere, with no instruction from the teacher about how or when they should happen. For instance, your class could be simulating a disaster relief team who are visiting an earthquake area. Suddenly, one of the children shouts out 'it's another quake!' and starts shaking. As if by magic, the other children join in one by one until the whole class is involved in simulating the earthquake.

Perhaps the best way to explain how simulations work, and how they might develop your children's creativity, is to give an example. The sample simulation below could be used for teaching geography at either primary or early secondary level.

Simulation: Pirate treasure

The teacher arrives dressed in a lab coat, dragging an ancient-looking chest which is padlocked shut. In character, she talks to the children:

Good morning and I'd like welcome you to our weekly meeting at the Museum of History. As you know, I am Sandra Smith and I am the Director here. Now, last night one of our workers found this chest in a dusty corner of the museum, but we can't seem to open it. In this morning's meeting we need to talk about what we do next. Does anyone have any suggestions?

At this point the children have been posed a problem — how to open the chest — and they can start to engage in some creative thinking and direct their own learning. If they immediately go for the most obvious answer — 'smash it open!' — the teacher might comment in character, 'but what if the contents are fragile, or even . . . dangerous?' Just a few of the other suggestions that might crop up would include:

- Hunt for the key
- Saw through the padlock
- Cut a hole in the side
- Take an X-ray of the chest to see what's inside.

From this point onwards the teacher will have an intention or objective in mind, and ways of facilitating those outcomes. However, to some extent (depending on how interesting their responses are) she should allow the children to guide the progression of the work. In this instance, the teacher's idea is that:

- The children do find a way to open the chest (the teacher has actually glued the key to the bottom).
- Inside they find a map giving the location of some pirate treasure. (Note: This could be an exotic overseas spot, but it could equally well have been buried in a position that turns out to be conveniently located in the school playground!)
- The class look at this map in detail, discuss what the landscape is like, where it might be, the geographical features they can see, and so on.
- The museum decides to pay for an expedition to find the treasure.
- The children work in groups to plan their journey, using maps, atlases and globes.
- They talk together to decide on the equipment that they will need to take.
- They are asked to think about how the landscape might have changed since the map was drawn many centuries ago.
- Depending on the particular geographical phenomena that the teacher wishes to study, she might for instance include a

river on the map and get the children to research how this might have changed.

- The class simulate their journey to the location, perhaps doing some freeze frames of moments of danger during the trip (having to fight with tigers may feature prominently).
- On arriving they use the map to locate the treasure. The teacher draws out the various geographical features in chalk on the playground floor for the children to explore and examine.
- If possible, the teacher buries a pirate chest in a corner of the school grounds for the children to find and dig up.
- Afterwards they make their own miniature treasure chests to bury in the school grounds, and draw their own maps to lock up in a secret place.

Ideas for simulations

To whet your appetite for this approach even further, and to help you come up with possible scenarios, below is a list giving lots of different ideas that you might use to develop a simulation in your own classroom/subject area.

- *Jobs/areas of professional expertise*: builder, doctor, nurse, carpenter, personnel director, spy, government scientist, TV presenter, journalist, farmer, ghost hunter, vet.
- *Time periods*: Ancient Greece, Tudor England, prehistoric man, 2,000 years in the future, in a museum, in a castle.
- *Settings*: the desert, under the sea, outer space, a hospital, a hotel, an office, a post office, a garage, a supermarket, a bank, an estate agency, a restaurant, a market, the seaside, an art gallery.
- *Problems*: stuck on a sinking boat, a building burning down, a crime scene, an injured animal, an aeroplane flying into a storm.
- *Fictional settings and characters*: Alice's Wonderland, the Three Little Pigs, Bob the Builder, Cinderella, Snow White and the Seven Dwarfs.
- *TV formats*: game shows, documentaries, soap operas, weather forecasts, dramas, adverts.

6 Blueprints for creativity

Only connect.

E. M. Forster

This chapter gives ideas for ways of developing children's creativity right across the curriculum and at a range of different ages. I can't possibly hope to do justice here to the intricacies and techniques of every individual curriculum subject at both primary and secondary levels. So instead I'm going to offer you what I call 'blueprints for creativity' – outlines of the sort of lessons that you might use to encourage greater creativity from your children, or ones that involve the teacher delivering them in a creative way. Many of these lesson ideas will work in more than one subject area, and can be adapted to suit children of varying ages or abilities.

The lessons that I present here are not 'lesson plans' as such, with lists of attainment targets that might be met or suggestions for cross-curricular links. Rather, they are simply the stories of some of the things that have happened in my own and other people's class-rooms, and examples of how the children have responded. Some of them are detailed and in depth; others brief. You will hopefully use your own imagination and creativity to adapt these in a way that suits you and your students.

Some of the lesson ideas in this chapter are my own, but a lot of what goes on in teaching is about the mixing up and sharing of what works best. Consequently, much of this material is 'borrowed' from elsewhere: from lessons that I've been lucky enough to watch; from ideas that I've been sent or told by other teachers; from INSET courses that I've attended; or from great ideas that I've spotted in books or on the Internet. I've acknowledged my sources where I know them or can remember them. However, if you spot any of your own ideas here, or if you have a great lesson that you'd like to see included in the next edition of this book, then please feel free to get in touch with me at sue@suecowley.co.uk.

The scene of the crime

This is a lesson with endless potential for developing creativity and creative thinking. I've used it myself for both English and drama, but it would work equally well in many other areas of the curriculum with small adaptations.

The teacher sets up a crime scene in a corner of the classroom, using a variety of props, some furniture and, if possible, some proper police crime-scene tape. (You can buy this on the Internet – it's quite expensive but well worth the money for the air of authenticity that it adds to the story. I buy mine from www.uktapes.com, who sell a range of tapes with great classroom potential – hazard warning tapes and so on.) The props that you use can be pretty much anything you might lay your hands on. I tend to set up the scene to look as though a card game has been going on, with a bit of gambling and drinking, and some mysterious items such as a computer disk or a key. If possible, it is great fun to add a real 'dead body' (a willing teaching assistant perhaps, or maybe a sixth former – in one instance I even borrowed a head teacher!). Alternatively, you could tape or draw the outline of a body on the floor.

When the children arrive at the classroom door, the teacher warns them that 'there's been a murder'. At this point, if any of your children take you a bit too literally, you can drop out of the story and let them know that it's only a fiction. The teacher asks the class to come inside, warning them to be careful not to touch anything, for fear of contaminating the forensic evidence.

The class gather in front of the tape for the teacher to introduce the lesson. She tells them that the police are very busy at the moment, and so they've asked that the children work as detectives and scenes of crime officers to help them solve the crime. Immediately, the class are motivated to find out what has happened. Their familiarity with the language and techniques of police work is most likely learned from television programmes, but it never ceases to amaze me how much knowledge they already have.

The teacher asks for a couple of volunteers to take a closer look at the crime scene. These students are given plastic gloves to wear to keep the crime scene 'clean' (you can buy these at the super-market). At this point you might also want to take some photo-graphs with a digital camera. The volunteers hold up the evidence and get the rest of the class to discuss what each piece might mean. By this point the children are often already busy inventing story-lines of their own to solve the mystery. (The most amusing that I've heard began something like this: 'Well, miss, there's a secret teachers' gambling den that goes on at lunchtimes – didn't you know? Some of the teachers meet up and play cards and drink as well. And what happened was Mr X got cross with Mrs Y because she called him a cheat . . .')

Once the children are all reasonably familiar with the crime scene, they are split up into small groups to discuss things further. Alternatively, the teacher might lead or facilitate a whole-class discussion about what has happened. The children have to apply lots of creativity to work out how to incorporate all the different bits of evidence into their stories. I tend not to set up the crime scene with one specific 'right answer' in mind, as this can mean that you end up looking for that answer rather than allowing the children to find answers of their own.

When some ideas about what has happened have been accumu-lated, the children are split into small groups to re-enact the crime to show the Chief of Police what might have happened. They practise their scenarios and then show these to the class, at this point using the actual crime-scene area and props during their performances.

There are plenty of options for work arising out of this scenario – interviewing witnesses and suspects, writing witness statements, drawing plans of the crime scene, and so on. You might use this idea as a starting point for work in many different curriculum areas. For instance, in an ICT lesson the students might find a disk with top secret information that must be decoded.

A game of cards

Cards, and card games, can be a brilliant resource to use in the classroom. The students see them as a bit 'adult', a little bit 'naughty', and you can use them to give rise to some great creative thinking.

One exercise that I do regularly using cards involves looking at status, and at how we treat other people. The thinking that comes out of this can also help your students explore the way that bullying makes others feel. Hand out cards to a small group of students, or to the whole class at once if you feel brave. Ask the children not to look at the card you hand them, but to hold it up against their foreheads with the picture facing outwards.

Explain to the students that the highest status or most important card is the king, with the ace being the very lowest, then 2, 3, and so on going upwards. They are going to move around the classroom and, when they pass another student, they must respond to him or her in the appropriate way. For instance, if they meet a king or queen, they should bend down and be subservient. On the other hand, if they come across an ace (1) or a 2, they should treat them badly.

Once the class have had a go at moving around the room and responding to the other students, ask them to try and line themselves up in the correct order from least to most important. Amazingly, in my experience most classes are able to do this almost perfectly. After finishing this exercise, you might talk with your children about how it felt to be a low number card and to be poorly treated by others.

In a maths lesson, you might use packs of cards to stimulate creative thinking about probability. Instead of leading the discussion yourself, ask the children to come up with various different ways of exploring probability using a pack of cards. They might suggest looking at the probability of turning over:

- A red or black card.
- An odd or even card (not as easy as it might sound – the children will have to realize that some cards might turn up that are neither odd nor even).
- A royal card.
- Cards from the different suits.

Characters on trial

This is a great approach for exploring characters in a story where a crime is committed. Ask your class to develop a proper trial, with prosecution and defence, witnesses, jury, judge, and so on. This is quite a complex process and you will need to do a number of preparatory lessons before the trial itself can take place.

Smartie probability

This lesson looks at probability: specifically the probability of the next Smartie out of the tube being a blue one. The children are asked to make suggestions as to how they might work out the likelihood of getting a blue sweet. They also make charts to show the number of Smarties of different colours in the tube, using squared graph paper and sticking on smartie shapes.

The horse race

This activity looks at odds and betting as part of a maths lesson. The classroom is set up as a racecourse, with various obstacles over which the 'horses' have to ride. Volunteers are then timed as they race around the track, and odds are set for each race.

Left luggage

When writing stories, our students will often rely on replicating characters that they have already seen on the television or read about in books. This lesson offers a great way to get your children thinking creatively. It encourages them to use their imaginations to develop interesting, original characters of their own.

Fill a bag (handbag, backpack, suitcase) with lots of different items. The contents can be pretty much anything you have to hand – keys, wallet, photograph, map, matchbook, crayon, computer disk, foreign coins – whatever you like, really. Try not to have too specific an idea of the bag's owner in your mind: the object of this exercise is not to find a 'right' answer, but a whole variety of potential ideas.

Show the bag to the class, and explain that it was found in the staffroom/classroom that morning. Tell the class that the police want to trace the owner of the bag, but they have no idea at all about where to start searching for this person. Ask the children to work as detectives to try and establish what sort of person might own this bag. I tend to talk through the contents of the bag with the whole class first, then ask the children to work individually or in groups to draw up their character sketches. They must try to explain the links they make between what is in the bag and the type of person they describe.

A variation of this exercise is to fill a suitcase with lots of one item, perhaps something bizarre, and to tell the class that it was left on the baggage carousel at the airport. (The teacher who gave me this idea had filled her suitcase with bananas!) The children then build a story from the strange contents of this suitcase.

A new coat of paint

The inspiration for this lesson came from the song 'New Coat of Paint' by Tom Waits. If you're a dance or drama teacher looking for inspirational tracks to develop creativity, I highly recommend this singer/songwriter's innovative work. The first step was to get the class to listen to the music: first time round, without asking for any specific response, then second time round getting them to note down some ideas and impressions.

After this, with the music playing quietly in the background, we talked about the kind of moods, images, characters, locations, etc. that the track brought into their minds. We also discussed some other 'paint' images, such as 'paint the town red'. The class then split up into groups and developed short scenes from these initial ideas, eventually incorporating props, costumes and furniture.

Location, location, location

This was a drama lesson concerned with developing and creating a sense of place and time. It was very much a brainstorming session, out of which came a flood of images and impressions that were later developed into more finished pieces. First, I simply asked the students to sit in a space, close their eyes and imagine a location. We started off with a prehistoric desert landscape, with me asking what they could see, hear, smell, etc. Afterwards we discussed the kind of images and sensory reactions that this brought up – these included fire, heat, animals, furs, chanting, hunting. Then we moved on to a New York street on a Saturday night. This time the sensory impressions were those of nightclubs, city sounds, taxis, traffic, police sirens, drunks, music.

Next we sat in a circle and brainstormed words. I gave a location and asked the students to say one word or phrase each as quickly as they could, around the circle, to create a stream of impressions. I used locations such as an emergency room in a hospital, a street in London when the end of the Second World War was announced, the moment after the assassination of President Kennedy.

After this the students got into groups and created a freeze frame of one location we had explored thus far. Going around the room, I got them to unfreeze and show a short piece of action (about ten seconds' worth), then freeze again. Staying in groups, we then moved on to some short improvisations incorporating a specific sense of time, and looking at how it related to character, mood and emotion. Again, I gave a range of settings for them to explore. We used:

- Trafalgar Square at 10 seconds to midnight on New Year's Eve.
- A nightclub at chucking out time.
- A changing room, one minute before the FA Cup Final.
- A changing room, one minute after losing the FA Cup Final.
- A spaceship, thirty seconds before an asteroid hits.
- A lift, three hours after breaking down.

Finally, we did a whole-class exercise that eventually resulted in some very powerful whole-class creativity. For this, the students had to lie down in a circle with their heads at the centre as close as possible, and their feet outwards. I then gave them some settings for which they had to provide a 'soundtrack'. These included a Victorian asylum, a prison in the build-up to a riot, and a rainforest just before a storm. At first, when using this exercise, the temptation was to make a cacophony of sound. Eventually, though, the students realized that for it to work they would have to contribute only as and when appropriate. The aim was to start quietly, rise to a crescendo, and then fade out, with the class stopping at exactly the same moment without any signal. I tape recorded some of these soundtracks for the class to listen to and use in their drama work.

Protest songs

This is an idea for a music lesson on protest music. The teacher sets up the classroom as a TV show, on which various guests have been invited to discuss their music. Guests (played by students) might include musicians such as Ms Dynamite, Bob Dylan, Bob Marley, Black Eyed Peas, Steve Earle, Billy Bragg, etc. A sample of the music of each singer/songwriter is played and discussed. The singers talk with the class about their ideas and their music (this involves quite a lot of research being done in previous lessons). The other students are then able to ask questions and respond to what has been said.

Flour babies

This work is inspired by the book *Flour Babies* by Anne Fine. It is useful for any work related to taking responsibility and also to looking at teenage pregnancy. I give each member of the class a bag of flour (use a supermarket value brand as these are only about 10p a bag). The students are then asked to treat these bags of flour as their 'babies'. They must take care of them for a set period of time – one week is about right. During this time, they must treat their babies as though they are real. This means that they must take their babies everywhere with them. As this will mean having them in other lessons, it is best to warn the teachers at your school beforehand. The students' responsibility is not just during school time: if they have to go out in the evening, then they must arrange for someone to babysit.

When using this activity I have found that some of my students respond with a great sense of creativity. I have even seen the bags of flour dressed up in knitted hats and booties, and with little faces drawn onto them. I have also asked my students to write diaries about their feelings and experiences during their time as parents.

Although it might seem like a recipe for disaster, this exercise has proved most successful for me when working with the most 'challenging' students. (In this instance, only one student disappointed when he locked his 'baby' in his locker for the entire week!) Surprisingly, in the 'nicest' school in which I have worked, there was a rather unfortunate incident immediately after the lesson when the babies were handed out. Several girls came to me in tears complaining that their babies had been 'kidnapped'. Shortly afterwards news reached me of the flour baby massacre that had taken place in the playground. I had a bit of explaining to do, but despite this disaster I'm still convinced that it's worth the risk taken in trusting your students.

A variation on this exercise is to give your children (hard boiled) eggs to look after for a day or so. Admittedly, these do start to smell a bit after a while.

Hunting Elmer

These cross-curricular activities arise from reading the *Elmer* books by David McKee. First of all get the class to cut out and colour some small Elmers, using squared paper. Next ask the children to make plans of the school nature area, if you have one, including the various geographical features. Then laminate the Elmers and set up an 'Elmer Hunt' by hiding them in the vegetation of the nature area.

At this point the 'Elmer Hunt' can begin. The children must mark the places where the Elmers are found on their maps. You might give a prize for the child who finds the most Elmers.

After the Elmer Hunt, you could go on to do some mathematical work based on the Elmers with their coloured squares, for instance counting the number of squares on each Elmer to calculate the total Elmer area. You might also create Elmer stories of your own, based on the day of hunting Elmers.

The Sand Horse

Many thanks to Suzy Edlin for sharing this story with me, which tells of her creative experiences while teaching in the Canary Islands.

The art project I was most proud of last year had an unusual start. It was with my Year 5 class and the objective was 'to tell a story through art'. Illustration being a passion of mine, I started off by showing the children lots of examples of paintings and textile work that portrayed a story, and then focused on a particular, favourite children's book of mine, *The Sand Horse* written by Ann Turnbull and illustrated by Michael Foreman.

I read the story and the children listened. I repeated the story and the children drew the images that came to mind as I read (they were not spectacular and, if I'm honest, rather predictable). Then we all looked at the illustrations and how the illustrator had supported the text and helped to tell the story. I then set the challenge for the half-term, which was to capture the *whole* story of *The Sand Horse* in one piece of artwork using fabric and batik techniques.

Now, Canarians are very expressive people generally; in speech, arms fly about and words are spat . . . and that's when they're happy! Yet, these kids were shocked at my methods of stiring up some enthusiasm for their challenge. I wanted to tap into their creative beings and get away from their premeditated ideas of what waves and horses look like. I split the class into three groups: one group had untuned musical instruments, those suitable for conjuring up the mood of the sea; another had an enormous sheet of paper laid out on the floor with a variety of brushes and sea-like colours of watered-down paint; the last group had whiteboard pens and were stood at the whiteboard, scribbling any words that they could think of that described the movement of the sea. The children then set to work and as one group played, one group painted and the other group wrote. The emphasis of the whole thing was on *movement*: I encouraged the painting group to paint using their whole bodies – knees bending, arms swinging, waists twisting, and so on (no delicate 'painting by numbers' here!); the writers fed in to the painters as I, expressively, read out what they were scribbling (again, pretty handwriting was not allowed); and the whole process was happening under an umbrella of sounds of the sea. After a while they all swapped around . . . because it's school and you have to give everyone a go!

The freedom of expression they eventually felt was wonderful. The place was buzzing. From that point on they embraced the challenge with their whole beings. While they then set to work in their pairs, reading the story and working out which images best captured the entire book, I worked with small groups of children giving them the chance to experiment with batik techniques. By the time it came for them to commit to an idea, they were all aware of the nature of batik and could select ideas that suited the medium.

Overall, this topic was a great success. The finished batiks were full of colour and movement – not a predictable, delicate, wave pattern in sight. My colleagues looked at me with a mixture of shock and, I like to think, awe! 'How does she get away with it?' was probably going through their minds. We were all splattered with paint and exhausted throughout, but it definitely loosened up the old creative brain-cells and got all the kids going for it, from the 'attention-seeking' trouble-makers to the 'oh, so correct' violinists! And we had fun, which at the end of the day is what it's all about.

I like to work BIG. My parting gift to the school in Gran Canaria was designing, drawing and enlisting the help of the secondary pupils in painting two enormous murals in the school playground. They were about 25 feet high, at least, and 40 feet wide I should think. For class assemblies I often get the children to make huge masks, out of bamboo and newspaper, which two or three of them can hold. I find something releasing about working big. Somehow, you have to bare your soul with large artwork. You can't cover it up with your arm, or hide it under a book. If it's big, it's going to be noticed, so you may as well put your heart and soul into it, make a statement and be proud of it!

Many thanks to Tim Gayler from Drayton School in Banbury for sending me the ideas given below. There can hardly be a better demonstration of how both teacher and students can approach science lessons in a creative and imaginative way! For more great ideas see the thread 'Making it fun' in the Science forum at www.tes.co.uk/section/staffroom.

Pouncing predators

(Inheritance and Selection – Key Stage 4)

The students get into groups of three. Two students go to the ends of a table, where both can reach into the middle. A pencil (representing prey – a dead gazelle or whatever) is put in between each pair on the desk. When the third person says 'go', both predators grab for the pen. They do this three times to decide a winner.

The winner from each group of three goes up against other pupils around the class. The teacher keeps emphasizing the point that unless you get the food you cannot survive/breed, etc. The overall winner then takes on the teacher (always worth a giggle). If you think you'll lose then you can suddenly have a mutation (i.e.

your hand is already stuck out over the pencil). I normally play with sweets rather than pencils. This exercise generally takes around 10–15 minutes with a group of 30 students.

The weakest vertebrate

(Classification – Key Stage 3)

A fun idea, with I must admit little educational value, to liven up classification lessons. First go to a joke shop and buy up their rubber insects, snakes, rats, etc. Have these in your pocket (I have a lab coat with large pockets that is ideal for this).

Start the lesson with the students gathered around the front. Talk about how we can look at animals to classify them, etc. and then say 'I've got some here'. At this point throw the rubber animals into class. Giggle massively as they scream. When they've calmed down you will have their complete attention, and will now be regarded as quite mad. (This worked best with very lifelike rubber cockroaches!)

In my own case this then led on to the following. The class were split into groups to discuss what made each vertebrate group special. Then one child from each group had to elect a 'head reptile', 'head amphibian', etc. This person was then 'hot-seated' and interviewed (in role) by myself and the class to try to determine what made them special. It went something like this: 'So Mr Fish: you can swim, that's nothing new . . . all the other groups here have swimmers. You are the weakest vertebrate, goodbye.' A great load of argument and discussion went on in this lesson!

DIY water cycles

(States of Matter – Key Stage 3)

A problem-solving lesson on 'making your own water cycle'. Give the students a range of equipment (both useful and non-useful), e.g. beakers, funnels, Bunsen burner, white tiles, cotton wool (this fools them into making clouds). The groups then have to construct a (safe) working water cycle.

If several groups get a water cycle working you can test each one by giving each group a measured amount of water. They must run their equipment for five minutes and then see how much water is left. The group with the most water wins.

Getting into the gut

(Digestion – Key Stage 3)

Get some chicken wire and poppit beads (the sort that pop together to make toy necklaces work well). Explain that enzymes are 'chemical scissors' (or whatever your stock phrase is) that can take apart large molecules for absorption (show linked poppit beads for a large molecule).

Get a student to come up to the front and ask him/her to hold up some chicken wire. Explain that this is the gut wall. Throw linked beads at this – they will not penetrate. Now show how an enzyme can cut up the large length of food molecule. Throw dissembled beads at the chicken wire again to show that some will now go through.

Alien impressions

(Metals – Key Stage 3)

Deeley boppers/flashing bunny ears are great for doing alien impressions. Teacher says: 'Tell me earthling, describe this thing you call metal or be disintegrated.' Child replies: 'Metal is heavy.' Teacher says: 'Ah, you say it's heavy? So this wooden table is metal . . . no it is not, you lie! DIE SCREAMING CHILD!' (Teacher makes raygun sound.)

Let's rock!

(Rock Cycle – Key Stage 3)

One revision demonstration that works well for the rock cycle is as follows. You will need: several pieces of chalk, a heat-proof mat, safety screens, a 250 ml beaker of water, a 100 ml beaker, and a hammer. The class should know the rock cycle already, and should be encouraged to talk/shout you through the cycle (with the teacher acting dumb sometimes). Here we go . . .

'Right you lot, starting with a piece of this rock [chalk], talk me through the rock cycle. [Students begin to describe cycle.] OK, weathering and erosion you say. We haven't got time for it to happen, so we'll speed it up. [Teacher hits chalk, which is on the heat-proof mat, repeatedly with hammer while grinning maniacally. Make sure the safety screens are up at this point.] Great, I enjoyed that. Now transportation. [The teacher washes the chalk dust down into a large beaker of water.] Now we can see it settling. [Pause.] That's boring; it's too slow. That's enough of that. Now we have cementation. This normally takes a very long time and a lot of pressure but . . . [Teacher rams small beaker into large beaker, water sprays out, compacted chalk dust is left at the bottom] look, here we have a new sedimentary rock at the bottom of the sea. Now, if the Earth moved up . . .'

No escape

(Space – Key Stages 3 and 4)

Here's a fun one for doing Space – orbits and satellites. Tie some rope (30-foot length) around a student's waist, holding the other end yourself. The teacher plays the Earth, the student is a satellite or incoming meteor, and the rope is the pull of gravity. The student has to try and run in a straight line past the teacher. When he tries, the rope will pull him into a neat circle around the teacher. This nicely reinforces some points about orbits after doing the swinging bucket of water over the head demonstration.

Sparking up

(Electricity – Key Stages 3 and 4)

An oldie but goodie. Demonstrate lighting a Bunsen burner with the spark from your finger after you've charged yourself up on a Van de Graff generator.

Magic moments

(Forces – Key Stage 3)

I've used this approach when studying moments with Year 9 students. Start off at the classroom door. Put the weakest student in the class right at the edge of one side of the door (furthest away from the hinge) pushing with one index finger. Then put the strongest student in the class on the other side of the door pushing with one index finger about two inches in from the hinge. When the teacher says 'go' both students push and the weakest one wins. Then add another student on the other side of the door and continue. See how many students you get up to on the strong side before the weak student begins to struggle.

Another option is to set up a ramp as a lever laid over a pivot on the classroom floor. The teacher stands on the very short end and the lightest student in the class is lifted (carefully), with support on each side, onto the other end. This in turn raises the teacher into the air . . . a magic moment indeed!

The hardest science teacher in school

(Forces – Key Stages 3 and 4)

Here's a great stunt that will impress your kids (though it's definitely not for the faint-hearted). Lay a finger flat on a table and pick up a standard can of beans (or any can of that sort of size), not SlimFast or any thicker-walled can. You are going to ram this down at speed onto your finger, but it will not hurt. Hold it so that the cylinder is horizontal (i.e. do not ram a flat end onto your finger – that hurts a lot!).

Make suitable martial arts noises, and windup attempts, then bring the can down at speed on your finger. The side will dent massively (I've even had one can burst doing this). At the most your finger will tingle a little (so far that's all that has happened at any rate). Glory in your new reputation as the hardest science teacher in school!

7 The creative school

One's destination is never a place, but a new way of looking at things.

Henry Miller

Of course, taking a creative approach to education cannot just be about individual teachers working in isolation in their classrooms. It is also about teachers working in tandem with each other, and about the school as a whole embracing these creative approaches. Building a creative school could be seen as a creative journey in its own right, and as we have seen throughout this book, that journey can be a long and complex one.

In this chapter I look at the various factors that go together to make a creative climate within a school. I examine what teachers, managers, other staff and students can do to help develop and sustain an ethos of creativity. I discuss ways in which the school environment can contribute to, or dampen, the creative spirit within a school's staff and students. I also look at the role of resources and displays in enhancing a creative feeling within a school. Finally, I look at the part that whole-school events might play.

A creative climate

In those schools where creativity thrives, the whole building will seem to buzz with energy and excitement. The children have a sense of purpose, high levels of personal fulfilment, and a feeling of being part of something bigger than their individual selves. Inside the classrooms, motivation is high and the students focus fully on their work. They enjoy their lessons, offering creative contributions to work in subjects such as science and maths, as well as the 'arts' subjects more traditionally associated with creativity.

The walls of the school are covered with colourful displays, and there are regular visits from artists working in many different fields. Beyond the school day, extra-curricular activities thrive, and school productions offer a public taste of the high quality music, art, dance and drama work that goes on during lessons.

A creative climate will not happen overnight, but small steps can be taken by any school with sufficient commitment to building a creative place. There are many different people involved in developing a creative climate in your school: not only the teaching staff and senior management, but also support and non-teaching staff, parents, and (of course!) the children.

When it comes to building a sustained creative climate, never forget that a group effort will typically be stronger and longer lasting than that of any one individual. Some schools will rely on one or two key creative individuals, perhaps a drama or music specialist who builds a thriving atmosphere of creativity over a period of time. However, things can quickly fall apart when that teacher moves on, so creativity must be more than a 'one stop shop' within a school. With a wider, whole-school emphasis on the value of creativity, the ethos of the place will quickly become much larger than any one individual.

Of course, with the development of more specialisms within education, it can be tempting to think that those schools who specialize in the performing arts should be the places where creative endeavours take place. However, as I hope you've seen throughout this book, creativity is not just of value in the traditional 'arts' subjects, but is of equal validity in science, the humanities, in fact in every subject taught within our schools.

Teachers in the creative school

To develop a creative climate, there will need to be individuals and teams of teachers who are interested in, and passionate about, extending creativity in their classrooms. Chapter 4 looks in lots of detail at the notion of the 'creative teacher'. In brief, though, this will mean teachers who:

- Look for creative ways to deliver the curriculum.
- Find opportunities for creative approaches as a normal part of their everyday teaching.

- Value the messy process of being creative, as well as the end result.
- Are willing to be innovative and take risks in their classrooms.
- Allow the children to take the reins, at least occasionally, when it comes to plotting and extending creative activities.

Managers in the creative school

Individual teachers can only do so much, though. If their efforts are to be a success, it is critical that they have the support of senior managers. This support could take various forms, and will include not only practical help but also positive attitudes towards creative approaches. As I hope I've made clear throughout this book, creativity can be a messy and risky business. If there is going to be genuine originality within a school, senior managers must maintain this support of their teachers when things go wrong as well as when they go right.

I've divided the advice here into various different categories. First and foremost, managers need to take a positive attitude to creativity if they want their schools to be truly creative places. If creativity is to happen for real, rather than being just another fashionable 'add on', there will need to be a change in mindset. Those who have been working in education for a long time may (after all those years of initiatives from above) find this quite difficult to achieve.

Attitudes to creativity

- Talking regularly to teachers about the help and support they really need, and asking for their ideas about how the school can develop its creativity.
- Encouraging and building a sense of teamwork between the teachers in the school – sharing good practice as often as possible.
- Giving creative activities a high profile within the school, and viewing them as an important part of what makes the school successful.
- Including details of, and an anticipation of, creativity in the relevant school policies. Making sure that these are not merely paper exercises, but that they genuinely filter down to, and influence, what actually happens in the classrooms.

- Valuing the messy processes of creativity as much as the end product, despite the fact that it is not so easily demonstrable to outside bodies.
- Offering staff the freedom and flexibility to adapt the curriculum to make room for more creative endeavours.
- Rewarding creativity in a public way – certificates, words of praise, displaying work, perhaps at a school assembly.
- Communicating and sharing their vision of creativity to parents. Ensuring that any parents who do work in creative fields are given the opportunity to share their work with the students.
- Daring to be different – refusing to let curriculum demands or fears about Ofsted reports dampen managers' and teachers' creative urges.

Managing time and timetables

- Exploring subject groupings and time allocated to different subject areas, to ensure that creativity is given sufficient focus, as far as possible within the constraints of the curriculum.
- Making time available for staff who wish to extend the children's (or indeed their own) creativity. For instance, giving teachers some non-contact time to work on experimental projects, or perhaps creating opportunities for teachers/ children in different classes to share their work with the whole school.
- Often, creativity will not fit into the brief periods of time that school lessons offer. Managers might take a creative look at how the timetable currently works, and consider whether teachers and students could be given a more lengthy period of time (e.g. a whole afternoon or day) for sustained creativity.

Managing the environment

- Analysing and adapting the school environment to maximize its creative potential (see 'A creative school environment' below for more ideas).
- Talking to teachers about how their teaching spaces aid or detract from the creative journey.

Developing staff creativity

- Ensuring that staff are given the time and money to access high quality training that inspires them to harness their own and their students' creativity.
- Using a staff meeting or some INSET time for all the staff to share their ideas about what 'a creative school' means to them.

Links across the school

- Finding ways of linking up different year groups in the primary school, or different subject areas in the secondary school.
- At secondary level, considering the ways that subjects are grouped. Would 'faculties' offer more likelihood of creative partnerships than departmental groupings? For instance, although drama is typically bundled in with English, it does in fact have far more in common with the other performing arts of music, art and dance.
- Incorporating plenty of creativity into assemblies. This might involve rethinking the typical content and delivery, from an information-based format to a more interesting, topic-led one.

Beyond the school day

- Supporting extra-curricular work and understanding the burden that this can place on staff.
- Thinking about holding whole-school events to celebrate creativity as an entire organization (see 'Whole-school events' below for more ideas).
- Supporting the wide range of teachers who get involved in working on school productions, whether this is through financial support, reduced timetable, encouraging full staff participation, etc.
- Working with outside organizations to help you become a more creative school, whether LEAs, local businesses, local media, other schools in the area (at the same and other levels), local colleges, local arts groups.
- Developing creative partnerships with local artists and organizations, and also across the country.
- Supporting teachers in organizing trips to theatres and other

creative venues. This should include museums and attractions dealing with science and other non-arts subjects, which take creative approaches to the teaching of science.

Managing budgets

- Supplying the financial back-up in terms of the diverse, quality resources that are needed for creative endeavours.
- Investing in technology that helps aid creativity.
- Paying to bring in expertise from outside the school, for instance theatre group workshops.
- Bringing working artists into the school – theatre groups, musicians, etc. and perhaps having an artist or writer in residence for a period of time.

Other staff

It is not only the teaching staff who build a creative buzz within a school. Clearly, teaching assistants and other learning support staff will need to play a key role within the classroom. These support staff must be included in all aspects of creative practice. But it goes much further than that. For many whole-school creative projects to take place, it will require the practical assistance (often beyond the call of duty) of a willing caretaker, helpful office staff, and so on.

It is worth thinking about how time outside of lessons can be spent in a more creative way, and liaising with the relevant members of staff to help this happen. This might mean discussing with catering staff their creative ideas for new menus; it could mean talking with playground supervisors about how the playground could be used in a more imaginative and creative way.

The students

It goes without saying that the students will play a crucial part in building a climate of creativity within a school. Pretty much all children will be happy to develop their creativity, so long as they are given the opportunity. Beyond the classroom, when it comes to building a more creative school, you might consider setting up forums at which your students can have their say. These could take the form of school councils, or some kind of student working party.

If these forums are to be worth while, the ideas that are developed need to have a reasonable chance of implementation. You might ask your children to talk about:

- What creativity means to them, and how well they feel the school is doing at the moment.
- Any ideas they have for developing creativity, both inside and outside the classroom.
- What goes on in lessons – which teaching approaches help them develop their creativity and how far they feel it is valued.
- Thoughts on how imaginative play could be incorporated into break times.
- The type of lunchtime and after-school clubs that they would like to attend.
- Any specific outside groups that they would like to see visiting the school (theatre, music groups, visiting artists, writers in residence, etc.).
- The type of equipment and resources that they need for greater creativity.

A creative school environment

I wonder that anyone does anything at Oxford but dream and remember, the place is so beautiful. One almost expects the people to sing instead of speaking. It is all like an opera.

W. B. Yeats

The environment in which we live will have a powerful influence on our experiences within that place. An open, sunlit room will put us in a very different mood to a dark, enclosed one. Similarly, a busy, urban landscape will imprint very different sensory experiences to a quiet, rural setting. Historically, many creative people have drawn inspiration from the environment in which they live: artists capturing the essence of a location with paint; poets distilling the sense of a place in words.

In the classroom, there are many factors that might inhibit creativity, both practical (elbows banging) and aesthetic (drab, peeling walls). Outside the classroom, some school environments are, to be honest, pretty stark and miserable. It stands to reason that our children are going to be affected by their environment in either a positive (creative) or negative (destructive) way.

When I go to visit schools, I am struck by all the efforts teachers and other school staff make to brighten up their environments. We are often fighting against almost impossible circumstances, and yet still that spark of creativity inspires us to fight against the dull or the depressing.

The way that our children react to and treat their environment is very telling. In some schools they interact in a very positive way, and are clearly proud of the place in which they study. In other schools they graffiti the walls of the toilets and pull down displays – a symbolic rebellion at a place that some see as a prison. The way that communal areas are kept must seem to our children to be an indication of how the school views their worth. Those teachers who work in these environments must wage a constant war against disaffection and for creativity, both in their children and in themselves as well.

On the subject of graffiti, this tradition might be turned to our advantage if we think creatively. Although it does damage the environment, it is still a form of self-expression. I've heard of some schools where they have dedicated a special wall on which the students are allowed to graffiti.

When they interact in a positive, creative manner with the very fabric of their school, our children build a special bond with the place. Our aim should be to make creative work a key part of the school environment, and to build a school that inspires every student towards creative learning. For instance, some schools have commissioned a sculptor or artist to make a work of art to put on permanent display either inside or outside the building.

Creative teaching spaces

That great cathedral space which was childhood.

Virginia Woolf

We spend our working days teaching in one space or another, but how often do we really look at them in any detail? It is well worth taking a bit of time to examine our various teaching spaces and to consider how we might make them more conducive to creative activity.

Inside the classroom

On the whole, teachers are stuck with the classroom or other space that they are given. Often it will be a case of making the best of what you've got (and that of course is where creativity comes in!). There are a number of factors that might mitigate against your children being creative. It is worth being aware of these and trying to keep any negative influences to a minimum. Below you'll find some problems and some creative suggestions as to how these issues can be overcome.

- *Lack of space, or an awkward-shaped room*: Try changing the layout of the desks, or perhaps dividing your room into different sectors.
- *Desks crowded together so that the students feel cramped*: If the desks are in rows, consider grouping them together. Check to see whether the layout would work better if you rotated it 90 degrees.
- *Room too hot or too cold*: If it's too hot, then open some windows and ask to get some blinds fitted. If it's too cold, get your students to wrap up warm and do some physical exercises between lesson activities. Check that the hot/cold levels meet with legal requirements.
- *Too much light or too little*: Again, if the light is too bright for your children to work, then ask that blinds be fitted. In a room with very little light, introduce as many reflective surfaces as you can (mirrors, silver foil, etc.).
- *A lack of decent resources*: Try to persuade the relevant manager that you're in need of some money from the budget to stock up. Teaching is probably the only job where people bring their own stationery to work, rather than 'liberating' it from workplace to home. Although I know I shouldn't have to do it, I'd rather buy the resources I really need than not be able to teach in the way that I want to.
- *Peeling paint or a dull colour on the walls*: If no one will answer your pleas for redecoration, then ask if you and your class can do it yourselves. Get the students to raise some money, and

then have a class 'paint in' one evening after-school. With 30 children it won't take long.

- *Displays falling down*: Stick them up regularly, with a staple gun if you're allowed. Every student I've ever known finds Blu-tack and drawing pins completely irresistible.
- *No displays at all*: Put some up asap! If you haven't got time or adult help, then hand this job over to the children. Any display is better than no display, even if it's just a few posters.

Outside the classroom

We often need plenty of space when we're being creative – not only in dance, drama and music lessons, but also for artwork. In curriculum areas outside the performing arts, you might need lots of space, for instance to get the children doing some large-scale experiments. Here is some general advice about the use of outside teaching spaces.

- *Share your open spaces*: The open spaces in our schools tend to have quite limited use in terms of the different curriculum areas. Halls, gyms, drama studios, playgrounds and school fields might be used regularly for PE, drama and dance lessons, but they can also be used for creative work in many different subjects. Of course, access to open areas will need to be scheduled, and first call will obviously go to lessons timetabled in these parts of the school. But I can guarantee you that the playground will be empty pretty much all day except for during break time. A quick trip outside is a great way to refresh your students and find space to let off some creative steam.
- *Share good management techniques*: Those teachers who are used to working in enclosed classroom spaces might have justifiable concerns about handling student behaviour within an open space. On the other hand, teachers who are experienced in managing children unencumbered by chairs and tables will have plenty of good tips. You might want to get together as a school to share examples of best practice. My own advice would be to:
  - Set very clear ground rules *before* you get into the open space – there is no way you will be able to get the class back if they decide to run away.

- Make it clear to the class that being allowed to use these open spaces is dependent on their good behaviour and work.
- Agree a signal for silent attention with the class – one that is easily seen or heard across a large open space (there's a good reason why many PE teachers use whistles!).
- Consider how and when you are going to move from your classroom to the open space. Set clear targets and time limits for the move, or it may end up wasting valuable lesson time. Alternatively, you might arrange to meet the class at the relevant place.

- *Don't forget the natural world*: Although quite a few playgrounds are a sea of tarmac, many schools will have a forgotten natural area that could be used to enhance creativity. In one school that I visited, almost an entire farm had been shoehorned into a small and fairly urbanized space. Get your children involved in making the most of the natural areas outside the school: there are plenty of opportunities for creativity and creative thinking in the art of gardening, for instance.

Resources for creativity

I'm well aware of how time consuming it is to keep resources sorted and organized. At times it can seem like a job that never ends, but it really is worth doing when it comes to enhancing your children's creative learning. For resources to work best in developing and reinforcing creativity, they will need to be:

- kept up to date
- well organized
- easily accessible
- accessible to all
- high quality
- diverse
- imaginative
- fun!

Many resources can be used right across the curriculum. For instance, a lot of drama departments or schools will have a costume and props cupboard of some kind. These costumes and props might usefully be incorporated into the simulation work that I talked about on pp. 93–102. If teachers are unsure about how to access and use these, then you might get a drama specialist at your school to do a short presentation at an INSET day or staff meeting, giving you lots of useful suggestions. Joke shops and party shops are also great places to find unusual resources.

Displays and creativity

The soul never thinks without a picture.

Aristotle

There are increasing moves to take the job of putting up displays away from the classroom teacher. This is great in terms of freeing up time, but personally I do find it just a little bit sad. Although they are time consuming to organize and put up, making displays is a creative and often enjoyable aspect of our work as teachers. Even if we are no longer responsible for physically putting up the displays, we will probably still play a part in deciding what goes into them and how they are designed. Here are some thoughts about the use of display work and the building of creativity.

- *Audit the current provision*: Take a detailed look at the display areas in your school as they currently stand. Consider how they are used by teachers and also how they are treated by the children. This will give you a good indicator of how positively displays are viewed. If you have a problem with graffiti, then this can be an indication that the children do not view display work in a positive manner. If teachers are not changing displays regularly, then it might be that children begin not to notice them at all.
- *Build shared spaces into the school*: There are often a large number of 'shared areas' within a school which offer great potential for display work. These might include a foyer area, the area just outside the school hall or dining room, walls in the corridors, and so on. Any area that gets a lot of traffic during the day will make a great place for the sharing of creative work. Ensure that the traffic is not just visitors to the school (as foyer or reception areas often are), but that the children themselves

regularly pass through and pause in these spaces. Consider whether you might put some seating into these shared spaces, to encourage the children (and indeed staff) to spend more time in them.

- *Don't forget the outside*: The external spaces at a school can offer plenty of space for creative displays. Nature areas, sculpture parks, and playgrounds might all be used to encourage creativity.

- *Consider your motivation*: Have a think about the motivation behind the display work that is done in your school. Is there a tendency to view it as wallpaper, getting it up as quickly as possible at the start of term and then leaving it up until it falls down? If teachers feel like this about displays, then the students will stop interacting with them.

- *Get the students involved*: Involve your children in any decision making that is done about the positioning and use of display areas.

Having taught at both primary and secondary levels, and being a regular visitor to schools in both sectors, I think it only fair to say that primary school teachers generally put their secondary school counterparts to shame in the display stakes. This is at least partly because they spend their time solely or mainly with one class, and there is perhaps more time and incentive to display the work of these students. If you are a secondary teacher and you are given the chance, then why not go to visit some of your feeder primary schools to see the work that is being done there?

For displays to be viewed in the most positive way, they must be:

- *Real and relevant*: Try to build a sense whereby displays are seen as an integral part of what goes on in the classroom and in the school as a whole, rather than as 'wallpaper' put up to make the place look 'nice' for outside visitors.

- *Interactive*: Those displays which encourage some sort of response from the children will help develop their creativity, and also make them more inclined to actually look regularly at what is on the walls. For instance, you might pose a question on your display board at the start of the week, and then ask the children to stick Post-it notes on with their replies to your question. You might also incorporate some multimedia effects, perhaps having a video loop running or a computer with a PowerPoint display.

- *Three dimensional*: We will often tend to use just the wall space for our displays. However, if there is room, put a table in front of the display area to exhibit lots of props and items related to the display. The children can then interact with these at relevant points during the lesson or day, with the teacher building these opportunities into the work.

- *Constantly changing*: When a display stays up for more than a few weeks, most of the children will have 'visited' it at least once. It might also start to look a bit tatty, and will probably no longer be reflecting the work that is currently going on in your classroom. Although it is inevitably time consuming, it is a great idea to try and change your displays regularly.

- *Inclusive*: Display work in schools needs to be inclusive – it should illustrate the work of all children who attend the establishment, rather than just a select few. Personally, I don't see what's wrong with the occasional spelling mistake on a piece of written work put up on display. However, if you can't bear to see spelling errors on your school walls, then the work can always be redrafted or typed up before being put on display. Ask the child to do this rather than doing it yourself – otherwise it becomes less 'their' work.

- *Appealing to all the senses*: Much of the time, schoolwork focuses on the visual to the exclusion of the other senses. The same will often apply to the displays we put up on our walls. However, there are plenty of ways in which we can get our children using all their senses. You might include some herbs which the children can crush and smell, or some different textures for them to touch.

Permanent displays

There will hopefully also be some opportunities for more permanent examples of your children's creativity to form part of the actual fabric of the school. Using this approach bonds the children to their surroundings in a very positive way. You might get a group or class of children to design and build a mural or mosaic, perhaps in conjunction with a local artist. You could ask some students to create sculptures that are put on more permanent display in a 'sculpture park' which forms part of the school grounds.

Whole-school events

When love and skill work together, expect a masterpiece.

John Ruskin

Whole-school events offer a great way to get all your students involved in a single creative endeavour. The positive outcomes that often arise from these events cannot always be easily measured. It is sometimes the case that the students' entire attitudes to school will change as a result of being involved in a whole-school event. As we saw at the end of Chapter 2 (see pp. 39–43), collaborative creativity is not necessarily easy to organize or structure. However, the more often children and teachers take part in group creativity, the more experience they will gain. Here are some ideas for whole-school events which celebrate and develop creativity.

- *Exhibitions*: Whole-school exhibitions offer a great way of sharing creative work with a wider audience. You might hold a school art exhibition which is open to parents and even to the general public. This exhibition might be a display of GCSE artwork, but it could equally well show the work of younger children or an entire primary school.
- *'Break out' or 'collapse' days*: This title makes these sound like days on which the students finally escape from the prison of school, or on which the teachers finally succumb to collapse. In fact, though, these are days on which the timetable is set to one side and the whole school comes together to undertake work with a common theme. The activities done on collapse days might come under the umbrella of one area of the curriculum, or run right across a range of different subjects. These days will often have a central theme, for instance I once worked on a 1950s' collapse day which we tied into a school performance of the musical *Grease*. These days can take a lot of organization and effort, and they need a head teacher who is willing to spend time away from statutory curriculum work. However, they are normally well worth it in terms of

increased motivation and creative outcomes. It works well to set up a series of rooms where different activities are taking place during the day, with a chance for the whole school to come back together at the end of the day to share ideas and experiences.

- *Play in a day*: I've used this activity as an option on a collapse day, and the end result was shared with the school on the last day of term. I got together a group of students who were interested in creating a 'play in a day'. Having given the group an initial structure within which to work, they were then able to contribute their own ideas and creative suggestions as to the content of the play. We had a brief rehearsal period before showing our work to the school. The sense of achievement in these students (by no means all 'high fliers') was palpable.
- *Book days or weeks*: An organization called Book Trust coordinates a National Children's Book Week in schools. During this time, lots of activities to encourage reading are arranged in schools throughout the country. For more information, see www.booktrust.org.uk.
- *Author days*: These are days on which the students and teachers look at the work of one particular author. In one school at which I worked, we organized a Shakespeare day. There were lots of activities based around Shakespeare's work, as well as performances by teachers and students alike.
- *'Real-life' careers day*: This is a careers day with a difference. Rather than simply handing out information about careers, the idea is to set up lots of different rooms where 'real-life' workplace scenarios are underway. This might include a hair salon, a building site, an office, a hospital, etc. Doing this gives the students a taster of what these jobs are really like. You might ask for parents or local businesses to send in some experts to help you with demonstrations, and get the students involved in actually trying out some of the skills that these careers demand.

In praise of whole-school productions

Pretty much the whole curriculum can be used creatively under the umbrella of a school production. Drama, dance, music and art are the obvious ones. But there are plenty of other opportunities for both children and staff to make a creative contribution. Here are some ideas.

- Design and technology: lighting plans, designing/building sets, making props.
- Textiles: designing and making costumes.
- Science: creating special effects.
- Maths: calculating ticket prices.
- Business studies: front of house and promotion.
- English: ticket and programme design.

Hand over the reins to the students as far as possible: you won't necessarily get such a polished and good-looking end result, but they will learn a huge amount. Although it would be a big undertaking, a whole-school production could actually be created by the students themselves, with a bit of guidance from their teachers. This would give real ownership of the piece and an incredible sense of creative achievement.

Appendix: Resources for creativity

Texts

Frames of Mind: The Theory of Multiple Intelligences – Howard Gardner
Use Your Head – Tony Buzan
Six Thinking Hats – Edward de Bono
The Creative Writing Coursebook – Edited by Julia Bell and Paul Magrs

All Our Futures: Creativity, Culture and Education
Anyone interested in the whole area of creativity within education (and indeed, beyond it) should read this report. It was published in 1999 by the National Advisory Committee on Creative and Cultural Education (NACCCE).

This report is available to download online at:
www.dfes.gov.uk/naccce/index1.shtml

Internet sites

www.ncaction.org.uk/creativity/index.htm
A website from the Qualifications and Curriculum Authority (QCA) giving practical ideas for developing creativity in the National Curriculum.

www.nonstopenglish.com/reading/quotations
An excellent searchable database of quotations for inspiration.

www.wisdomquotes.com
Another good database of inspirational quotations.

www.mind-map. com
Official website for Tony Buzan.

www.edwdebono.com
Official website for Edward de Bono.

http://pzweb.harvard.edu/PIs/HG.htm
Information on Howard Gardner.

www.creative-partnerships.com
A government-funded website/organization aimed at developing children's creativity.

See projects taking place in schools from different areas of the country.

www.sln.org.uk/art/p7.htm
Ideas for having an artist in residence – contacts and practical help.

Index